Modern Japan

A Captivating Guide to Modern Japanese History, Starting from the Period of the Tokugawa Shogunate through the Meiji Era and Imperial Japan to the Present

Free Bonus from Captivating History (Available for a Limited time)

Hi History Lovers!

Now you have a chance to join our exclusive history list so you can get your first history ebook for free as well as discounts and a potential to get more history books for free! Simply visit the link below to join.

Captivatinghistory.com/ebook

Also, make sure to follow us on Facebook, Twitter and Youtube by searching for Captivating History.

Table of Contents

Introduction

For over one thousand years, the samurai ruled Japan. These men were the warrior and governing elite of Japan from the middle of the 7th century CE until the mid-19th century. As you may know, the word "samurai" means "to serve." The original intent behind the word may have been that the samurai were supposed to serve and protect the people. However, by the time the country united behind one man in the early 1600s, the samurai were mainly serving their lords and attempting to keep the rest of the Japanese population in its place. Unfortunately, that is all most people outside of Japan know about Japanese history, with the possible exception of Japan's role in World War II.

Captivating History's *Modern Japan* takes you on a journey back through time to the days when feudal lords battled one another for control. We will see the emergence of modern Japan in the 1870s, its amazing rise to power, and its devastating defeat in WWII. Then, we will explore present-day Japan, which is one of the most economically powerful nations on Earth.

This book is an introduction to modern Japanese history, so it is relatively short. But don't let the brevity of the book fool you! Inside this volume, you'll find more than facts and figures. You'll read about the Sengoku Jidai ("Warring States period"), the one-hundred-odd years of constant civil war that finally culminated in a united nation. You'll have a deeper understanding of some of Japan's more unique practices, from the ritual suicide practiced by the samurai to the incredible beauty of a tea ceremony and the unique Japanese poetry form known as haiku, along with much else.

If you missed or didn't have the opportunity to learn about Japan and its history and culture in school, Captivating History's *Modern Japan* will fill in the gaps between the samurai and the incredibly modern and influential nation that Japan is today.

Let's start with some simple facts and figures that might help you understand some aspects of Japanese history and culture.

Japan is 146,000 square miles in area. It is just a bit smaller than the US state of California, which is nearly 164,000 square miles in area. The population of Japan in 2020 was 126 million. In that same year, California's population was just under forty million—a difference of eighty-seven million people. From there, it's easy to find the population density per square mile or at least a close estimate. California, which is the seventeenth most densely populated US state, has 254 people per square mile. Japan has just under 870 people per square mile. While Japan does not have the densest population per square mile, it ranks thirteenth, and many of the countries ahead of it are either small islands or city-states, with a couple of notable exceptions.

This is a bit misleading, for Japan has a number of features that limit where people can comfortably live. Japan is a mountainous volcanic series of islands, so the amount of arable land (land that can be farmed) is very limited. Thus, Japan is home to some of the largest cities in the world, Tokyo being the prime example. Tokyo is made up of twenty-three wards and has a population of just over thirteen million people. When you take into consideration its immediate and dependent suburbs, that number rises to nearly *thirty-seven million*! That means that one in four Japanese live in or near Tokyo. It is incredibly crowded.

In 2000, I had the good fortune to travel to Japan as part of an educational exchange program. A group of American teachers from all fifty states traveled to Japan to learn about their education system and were given the opportunity to live in a Japanese community for a time in order to become better acquainted with both Japanese schools and Japan itself.

On one of our days off, I decided to walk across downtown Tokyo from my hotel to the Imperial Palace. The streets are clean, orderly, and incredibly safe, but they are crowded. By the end of a long day, I decided to take the train back to my room rather than walk. When I arrived at my station, the tremendous sense of claustrophobia I had been fighting all day finally hit me. Everywhere I looked, there were people; it was difficult to see the walls and floors of the station. What's more, most of these people were moving—literally thousands of them before my eyes. I had to get out! I went to a kiosk that had signs in English that said they assisted travelers, though the guide's English was not very good. However, after seeing the look on my face and hearing the one word that told her where my exit was, she led me not only out of the station but down the street outside and pointed to my hotel. I have rarely been more grateful to anyone!

After some rest, I realized that during that entire adventure, not one person had more than brushed passed me lightly. Every single person I spoke with, even though they could not understand me, stopped for a moment and tried to help, all accompanied by the most famous Japanese gesture, the bow.

There are many reasons for this politeness and hospitality, but why did I tell you that story after explaining the population of Japan? Can you imagine what Japanese society would be like if the people weren't polite and didn't have many unsaid "rules" about personal interactions? Japan would constantly be in chaos.

For those regular readers of our Captivating History series, you may notice that this book is a bit more detailed in the beginning chapters than those that follow it. That's by design. Japan's situation in the world before its opening to the West in the last half of the 1800s is unique in history. As you will see, the nation remained in self-imposed isolation for about 250 years. When US Commodore Matthew Perry forced Japan to open to the world in 1854, he found a nation frozen in time. Over the course of the next fifty-plus years, Japan transformed itself from a nation ruled by an ancient warrior elite class (the samurai) to a democracy. Without an understanding of that period, it is decidedly difficult to understand modern Japan.

Of course, there is much more to Japanese culture and history than the samurai and the fact that it's crowded. We hope that by the end of this short introductory book, you will both understand and want to learn more about this fascinating country and its people. To further your journey, please see the bibliography at the end of the book.

Chapter 1 – Tokugawa/Edo Period (1603–1867)

If you know a little about Japan but don't recognize the words in the chapter title, you likely know them by another name. "Tokugawa" is the name of the clan that claimed the title shogun ("barbarian-conquering generalissimo"), which might be familiar to you from the many books, anime, and movies on the subject of feudal Japan. Shogun was also the name of an amazing bestseller in the 1970s, which gave rise to renewed interest in Japanese culture, especially in the United States. In 1980, a mini-series starring Richard Chamberlain and one of Japan's most renowned actors, Toshiro Mifune, was one of the most-watched mini-series then and for years after.

You also know the city of Edo, as it is one of the world's great cities. Today, the city is known as Tokyo.

The book and series are loosely based on the story of William Adams, an English pilot working aboard a Dutch ship when it shipwrecked in Japan in 1598 on a trade mission to unlock Asian trade for Holland. Adams and the surviving members of his crew were imprisoned in Osaka Castle, which was under the control of the great general (but not yet shogun) Tokugawa Ieyasu. (As a note, Japan uses the convention of family ("last") name first and the given ("first") name last.)

At the time, the only foreigners allowed to trade with Japan were the Chinese and the Portuguese (the latter of which was zealously Catholic at the time and at war with the Protestant English and Dutch). The Portuguese controlled much of the trade coming from their new colony of Macau off the coast of southern China. Tea, silk, ivory, porcelain, art, and much else passed through Macau. And all of these items were in high demand in Japan.

The arrival of Adams opened the eyes of the future shogun, who was told much about Europe and the known world by William Adams. Much of what Tokugawa Ieyasu heard dismayed him. Considerable portions of the world outside Japan and Portugal's attitude and plans for Japan had been omitted by Japan's business partner. At the time, Portugal was one of the richest and most powerful nations on Earth.

Adams and one other man were kept in Japan as involuntary "guests" of the future shogun, while two of their compatriots were sent home to Holland to open trade negotiations. At the time, and for some time to come, the journey from Japan to Europe took over two years. That gave Adams plenty of time to help Ieyasu design a Western-style ship. (He actually designed two, one that was 80 tons and another weighing 120 tons. Both of them were used for coastal patrols.)

Adams was never allowed to leave Japan. Eventually, he was given the honor of being named a part of the samurai class for his services to Tokugawa Ieyasu. These services included the furtherance of Dutch and English trade in Japan and leading Japanese diplomatic and survey expeditions to what are today Thailand and Vietnam.

Adams became so vital to Tokugawa's information and diplomatic network that he had virtually unrestricted access to Japan's most powerful man until the death of Ieyasu in 1616. Adams died in Japan in 1619.

Tokugawa became the shogun in 1603 by aligning himself with two powerful generals in the later years of the Sengoku Jidai ("Warring States period"). Japan had essentially been at war with itself for over one hundred years. Regional lords (known as daimyo) fought one another for control of a territory or to increase their territory. Other factors, such as a personal vendetta, honor, and trade, could also be involved. This period began in 1467 with the fall of the Ashikaga clan, whose members were the shogun before the Tokugawa clan in 1603.

Tokugawa Ieyasu was actually brought up in the house of a rival clan, the Oda, as a hostage. The Oda, in turn, sent him to another clan, again as part of a hostage agreement (these usually took place to ensure the fulfillment of a promise or policy between samurai clans). Ieyasu lived there until he was fifteen, which was considered the age of adulthood.

"Hostage," in this case, does not mean that the future shogun was kept in a dungeon or a hole in the ground. Like similar situations in feudal Europe, hostages held by rival clans were treated almost like family; to not do so was less than honorable and could provoke a violent response. Young Ieyasu was taught all the necessary skills to be a fully-functioning member of the highest class in Japan, the samurai. This meant he trained in the arts of war, which included not only swordsmanship and archery but also strategies and tactics. The samurai were also expected to learn about the issues of the day, Japanese history, mathematics, and much else. For instance, the arts were stressed; a true samurai was a calligrapher and poet or sometimes a visual artist or a musician. When Tokugawa was released as a hostage at fifteen, he excelled at all of the arts of war and many of the artistic forms valued by the samurai.

Shortly after his release, the clan that had held him hostage was defeated by the Oda clan, and Ieyasu swore loyalty to them. This was an important decision, as a member of the Oda clan, Nobunaga, would become one of Ieyasu's mentors in warfare and politics. He would come close to ruling the entire country.

Illustration 1: Tokugawa Ieyasu as Shogun

Tokugawa Ieyasu was given Mikawa Province to rule as daimyo. Mikawa is about 160 miles southeast of present-day Tokyo. In the 1570s, Tokugawa Ieyasu fought a powerful neighbor, Takeda Shingen, on behalf of his overlord, Oda Nobunaga, who was on a truly bloody mission to unify Japan under his own rule. Though Ieyasu was defeated a number of times by the skilled Takeda Shingen, he acquitted himself well. In the end, with the help of Nobunaga, Ieyasu defeated Takeda Shingen. The next year, 1573, Takeda Shingen died (the circumstances surrounding his death have not yet been determined). With the defeat of the powerful Takeda clan, Oda Nobunaga was briefly the ruler of most of Japan.

Japanese history counts Nobunaga as one of three "Great Unifiers" of Japan. In one of the most infamous episodes in Japanese history, Nobunaga was assassinated by one of his generals, Akechi Mitsuhide, in June 1582 while staying overnight in a temple in Kyoto for a much-anticipated tea ceremony. Nobunaga believed himself secure since he was deep in his own territory and in the company of only some advisers. Mitsuhide deceived his troops into believing that their (and Nobunaga's) enemy was at the temple called Honno-ji. When they were just outside the temple, Mitsuhide announced his true purpose. He sent some troops to another temple and besieged Nobunaga inside the Honno-ji temple.

A one-sided fight occurred, with Nobunaga and a loyal retainer trapped inside a room. Nobunaga committed seppuku (suicide by self-disembowelment). (The popular hara-kiri is considered less refined and means "belly-cutting.") Before doing so, Nobunaga left instructions to his retainer to burn his body to prevent its capture. The retainer, Mori Ranmaru (a folk hero in Japan to this day), set fire to the building and then killed himself.

Akechi Mitsuhide attacked and defeated Nobunaga's son and his troops. Both father and son committed suicide when a defeat was obvious. Nobunaga's general, Toyotomi Hideyoshi, the second "Great Unifier," ended his campaign against a rival clan and defeated Akechi Mitsuhide one month later.

Hideyoshi, who had actually been raised from a commoner rank for his martial skills on and off the battlefield, was a brilliant general who fought against the man who would become the eventual shogun, Tokugawa Ieyasu. From 1582 to the early 1590s, Hideyoshi solidified his power through the distribution of spoils, land, positions, and outright fear. However, by the late 1590s, the daimyo who were loyal to him became more and more restless, as the lack of war meant the lack of spoils. This, combined with Hideyoshi's "common" ancestry, caused discontent that threatened his rule.

To both distract and cement the daimyos' loyalty, Hideyoshi invaded Korea. The campaign was a disaster. Intense Korean resistance and Chinese troops made the fighting on land difficult. Korea's navy was led by an admiral that would never know defeat: the Korean national hero Yi Sun-sin. The defeats on land, the lack of spoils, disease, and the cutting off of much-needed supplies meant that the Japanese were destined to be defeated. Hideyoshi could not announce Japan's withdrawal from Korea, knowing what such a move would mean for his prestige, but fate stepped in. On September 18th, 1598, Hideyoshi died. His death was kept secret by the now-ruling Council of Elders, and the Japanese troops were ordered home from Korea.

Over the course of the next two years, the leading daimyo of Japan struggled for power. While many supported Hideyoshi's infant son, who was represented by a regent, others threw in with Tokugawa Ieyasu, whose troops had not gone to Korea but had remained home to police the central part of Japan. In October 1600, Tokugawa Ieyasu won the Battle of Sekigahara. one of the most famous and pivotal battles in Japanese history. Over the next three years, Ieyasu solidified his power, and in 1603, he was named shogun by the emperor. He became the generalissimo of all Japan, something that Nobunaga had rejected (he did not want to be seen being "given" power when he had it) and that Hideyoshi was unable to secure due to his common birth. In Japanese schools to this day, students are taught a short saying to help them remember the names and order of the three "Great Unifiers." "Tokugawa ate the pie that Nobunaga made and Hideyoshi baked."

Illustration 2: Contemporary depiction of the Battle of Sekigahara.

Tokugawa Ieyasu was the first of fifteen Tokugawa shoguns. He ruled from 1603 to 1616. In 1605, he named his son Hidetada as his successor but held the reins of power until the day he died. Ieyasu laid the template for the next two hundred years of Japanese history.

Ieyasu's many accomplishments included the strengthening of the centralized state by imposing a nationwide tax system, a set of national laws, and the formal division of society into classes. The class system had many nuances, but at its most basic, it divided Japanese society into two classes: the samurai and everyone else.

At this time, wearing two swords became not only a privilege of the samurai but also a requirement. In 1588, Hideyoshi began what is called the "Great Sword Hunt," in which Japan's villages were combed for weapons held by peasants and other non-samurai. With the codification of the two-swords rule and the class system, the possession of any weapon by anyone other than a member of the samurai class was punishable by death—as were most other crimes. Most times, a samurai accused of a crime was given the opportunity to commit seppuku. In the Tokugawa era, a person was rarely found innocent after being charged. Even the rumor of law-breaking was enough to cause a man or woman (samurai women, although few in number, committed suicide by slashing or stabbing their throat) to commit seppuku. The penalty for criminals outside the samurai class was often public crucifixion.

One of the most vexing questions for the Japanese in the late 1500s and into the first decades of the Tokugawa bakufu ("bakufu" is a military term that literally means "tent" or "military government") was the arrival and presence of European powers.

The first Europeans arrived in Japan by accident. Three survivors from a Portuguese ship that had sunk in a storm came ashore on a small island off Kyushu, one of Japan's four main islands.

By 1547, the Portuguese, already having explored much of the previously unknown world (to Europeans, that is), had inserted themselves into Asian politics. Many years before the arrival of the Portuguese, an economic disagreement between the Chinese and Japanese essentially forced Japan into becoming a tributary state of China. This situation continued on and off for years, depending on the relative strength or weakness of the respective governments. But when the Europeans arrived in 1547, the idea that Japan was a tributary state to anyone was disagreeable in the extreme.

By the 1570s, the Portuguese had stepped in, acting as middlemen between the two empires and making a hefty profit along the way. They also established local dominance of the sea between Japan and China with their (for the time) modern ships, which were more advanced in virtually every conceivable way than those of the Japanese and Chinese.

The Portuguese brought the most popular Chinese trade good, silk, along with much else, to Japan and returned to China with ships full of gold and silver, both of which Japan had in abundance at the time. Of course, a considerable portion of that gold and silver went into Portuguese coffers. A share inevitably went to the Vatican, for it was Pope Alexander VI who had laid out the division of the New World between Spain and Portugal in the Treaty of Tordesillas in 1494. The contents of the treaty were kept a secret from the Japanese for many years. It essentially "gave" Japan to the Portuguese, something the Japanese would not have tolerated—and did not when it was discovered years later.

The Portuguese had two main goals: to make money and to spread Christianity. In 1549, one of the original members of the Jesuit Order, Francis Xavier (who is a saint in the Catholic Church), built the first Christian church in Japan. This was located in the town of Yamaguchi on the main island of Honshu, about halfway between the famous city of Hiroshima and the tip of Kyushu. Today, the site is Francis Xavier Park, and a memorial to the monk stands there today.

However, within a short time, many powerful Japanese became concerned about the spread and influence of the Christian faith, most notably Toyotomi Hideyoshi, the second "Great Unifier" of Japan. By the time Hideyoshi decreed a ban on Christianity in Japan, an estimated 100,000 Japanese had converted, including a number of influential daimyo in the south of Japan. They were mostly from Kyushu, the home of the port of Nagasaki, where the Portuguese did their trading.

While this ban forbade Christian missionaries (both Japanese and Portuguese) from spreading their beliefs to places in Japan other than Kyushu, it did not completely forbid the religion. Hideyoshi needed the Christian daimyo to both keep an eye on the foreigners and keep him in power.

To make clear what might happen to any Japanese that might be thinking of conversion, to discourage those already converted from spreading the word, and to send a strong message to the Portuguese, Hideyoshi had twenty-six Christians arrested in Nagasaki: three Japanese Jesuits, seventeen ordinary Japanese believers, and six Franciscan monks (including one from Mexico). The Franciscans were chosen deliberately. They were a rival order of the powerful, rich, and influential Jesuits. While there were Jesuit victims, they were purposely Japanese; legally, the Portuguese had no rights over them. This sent a message to the Jesuits, essentially telling them, "You are rich, and we depend upon you and your countrymen for trade with China, but this is a line you should not cross. These missionaries are Franciscan, but you could be next."

The message was a strong and extremely violent one: the twenty-six were put in small cages and paraded through Kyushu. Along the way, they were beaten and mutilated but left alive so they could be publicly crucified when they returned to Nagasaki.

In 1570, the Japanese confined most foreigners living in Japan to an island (Deshima or Dejima) off Nagasaki and only allowed diplomatic or trade missions to other parts of Japan on rare occasions. Goods were brought to Deshima from all over Asia, but it was the Japanese who sold them to the rest of Japan. This also served to put some control on the spread of Christianity, especially after the killing of the Twenty-Six Martyrs of Japan, as they are known today.

In 1600, as Tokugawa Ieyasu was coming to power in Japan, another group of foreigners, the Dutch, arrived. By this time, the Japanese had seen the Portuguese and the Catholic Church come to dominate pockets of China, and the Spanish Catholics had already conquered and begun to convert the Philippines. The Dutch were Protestant and were less interested in converting the Japanese to their religion than they were in trade and in weakening Portuguese and Spanish power and influence in Asia.

By 1614, Tokugawa had begun to see the spread of Christianity and the growing power of the Europeans as a threat, not only to his regime but also to Japan and its culture. The worst "offenders" (in the eyes of the bakufu) were the Portuguese and Spanish, whose intent to divide the world had been made clear to Tokugawa by the Dutch and the Englishman William Adams. Tokugawa ordered them to leave Japan and never return. The Dutch were allowed to remain only on Deshima to trade and had to keep their numbers small.

Tokugawa's third son, Hidetada, became shogun in 1605, though his father retained the real power as ogosho ("retired shogun") until 1616. Hidetada, who was in power from 1605 to 1623, continued most of his father's policies. After he retired, he became the ogosho to his son Iemitsu. Hidetada enforced increasingly anti-Christian acts and orders, including forcing daimyo who would not renounce Christianity to commit seppuku. He forced ordinary Japanese Christians to renounce their faith or be crucified and killed fifty-five Christians who refused to do so in Nagasaki in 1628. These victims were publicly burned.

In 1638, Christianity was officially outlawed in Japan by the third shogun, Tokugawa Iemitsu, who had issued a previous decree in 1635 that was to shape and control Japan and its culture for over two hundred years: the policy of *Sakoku* or "locked country." This is also known as Japan's period of isolation. This policy of isolation, though it did have occasional exceptions, kept Japan in a sort of time warp for the next two hundred years.

There were three principal reasons for Iemitsu's decree: limiting foreign influence (religious, economic, and cultural), cementing the Tokugawa bakufu (though the word literally means "tent," its primary meaning is "regime"), and keeping Japan "Japanese." As you read above, many Japanese, especially Iemitsu and those in the Japanese imperial family in whose name the shogun ruled, worried that the religious influence of the foreigners would translate into both political and economic power.

The Catholic powers in Asia, Spain, and especially Portugal were completely cut off from dealing with or in Japan. In their place, the Dutch, who showed virtually no inclination to convert the Japanese, were limited to islands in Nagasaki Bay. Japanese customers came to them rather than the other way round. The important China trade, while done to a degree with the Dutch, was mostly carried out through the Japanese vassal kingdom of the Ryukyu Islands (you likely know the main island, Okinawa). Trade with Korea was done through a Japanese-held island off that kingdom's southern coast. Trade was also conducted with the native Ainu people, who at the time were, for the most part, allowed a degree of autonomy in the lands of Japan's mountainous far north.

Throughout Japan's history, the Japanese have valued their unique culture, which developed as a result of the isolation afforded them by the ocean and the lack of any real ocean-going vessels visiting their shores other than from China and Korea. Though influenced by Chinese philosophy, culture, modes of dress, and more, the Japanese truly developed a distinctive culture, which led many to believe that the gods had created the Japanese islands and shepherded the Japanese into a unique and valued place in both the world and the heavens. The Europeans and their religion, economic power, and weapons threatened this worldview.

When the Europeans first arrived in Japan, Tokugawa and some of the more forward-thinking daimyo and samurai quickly realized one thing: the foreigners' weapons could dominate the battlefield. To that end, they not only purchased firearms (which were mostly muskets and pistols, as the Europeans were not inclined to sell the Japanese advanced cannons) but also hired Europeans to train some of their troops in the use of these modern weapons. Within a short time, the Japanese had reverse-engineered these weapons and their ammunition and began to create their own firearms.

By 1635, the Japanese had experienced the spread of Christianity and had seen the Europeans grow in strength, influence, and even direct control in Asia. Even if the shogun were able to limit the Europeans' religious and military influence directly, the Europeans' ability to travel freely in Japan would "pollute" the unique Japanese culture that had grown over the last thousand years.

Conversely, any Japanese traveling outside the islands could possibly bring home new ideas and practices, which threatened Japanese culture and the status quo politically. Foreigners were kept in virtual quarantine in Nagasaki Bay, and all Japanese were forbidden, on pain of death, from attempting to leave Japan. Those who did, including those already overseas on economic or diplomatic missions, were forbidden to return.

After Ieyasu, his grandson, Iemitsu, was the most influential of the shoguns. In addition to the policy of isolation, the third shogun further centralized power within Japan from the top down. The primary method used to increase control was taxation in many forms. Taxes were more effectively collected and administered than they had been under Ieyasu. An increasingly efficient centralized bureaucracy not only administered taxation but also developed a postal system and a system to improve infrastructure, especially the five main "highways" of Japan, most notably the Tokaido road, which connected the capital Kyoto to Edo to the southern regions.

Not only were the Japanese forbidden to travel overseas, but most Japanese, including most samurai, were also required to get travel permits if they were going to move from one region to another. This could take ages to obtain, especially if one had to travel through multiple regions under different daimyo. Incredibly, wheeled travel was forbidden. Carts to carry goods were allowed, although they had to be led, but anything resembling what was known in the West as a carriage or coach could not be used. Important persons rode horses or were carried by palanquins. Traders carried goods on their backs.

Much of the shogun's power was dependent on the loyalty of the daimyo and their retainers (samurai). To this end, Iemitsu put into place a unique system to control them, which lasted until the end of Japan's isolation in the mid-19th century.

First, the daimyo were required to assign a number of samurai to certain tasks set by the bakufu. Second, daimyo were only allowed to build one castle in their domain, whereas before, multiple castles were allowed, as they provided defense and prestige. Third, and most importantly, all daimyo were required to spend every other year in Edo as a "guest" of the shogun. (Edo was not the official capital of Japan; Kyoto was. However, Edo was the seat of power, so it essentially acted as the capital.)

This policy, known as *sankin kotai* ("alternate attendance"), meant that in addition to spending a year away from their domain, which would be perhaps administered by an underling closely watched by officials of the bakufu, the daimyo would spend much of the other part of the year traveling, depending on their proximity to Edo. The daimyo farther from the de facto capital of Japan were traditionally more rebellious and less trusted, so this was clearly intentional.

Not only were the daimyo to spend every other year in Edo, but their families were also to accompany them. All expenses were to be paid by the daimyo unless he was being granted a special favor or honor. He would also be expected to dress and feed himself, his family, his samurai escort, and occasional guests from his own pocket. If he ran out of money, that could easily be solved: borrow it from the bakufu at high interest. As you can likely surmise, this put many daimyo directly into the shogun's debt.

The daimyo's family, which often included his wife, mistress(es), and his heir, would be treated with the utmost respect, but the threat was obvious: misbehave, and your family will suffer.

Today, we would likely call Iemitsu a paranoid megalomaniac, and he became increasingly more paranoid and concerned with centralizing power as his reign went on. Despite this, some of his more extreme measures continued until almost the end of the Tokugawa shogunate, though in the latter part of Tokugawa rule, these strict rules caused increasing numbers of revolts, both among the samurai and the peasantry, the latter of which made up the vast majority of the population and whose numbers grew exponentially throughout most of the Tokugawa period.

His strict rules included the following:

- Carrying or possessing weapons of any kind was forbidden, except for the samurai, who were required to carry two swords (one long and one short). Both in times of peace and of revolt, "weapon hunts" were carried out in towns and villages. Anyone violating this rule was killed, often by crucifixion.

- Peasants were rarely allowed to leave the land they tilled or the town or village they lived in. If they did, they would be sentenced to death.

- Buddhist monasteries, which had often been sources of revolts prior to Ieyasu and which had been ruthlessly punished because of them, were brought back. They were under strict government control and had to profess their absolute loyalty to the shogun (and, through him, to the emperor). The same held true with Japan's native religious beliefs, known as Shinto, which at the time was seen as an upper-class imperial belief system. Shinto, generally speaking, is a religion unique to Japan and consists of the worship of various gods and goddesses, as well as ancestor veneration. Most Japanese today identify as both Shintoists and Buddhists to one degree or another.

These are only three of the draconian decrees put into place by Iemitsu. As time went on, they became institutionalized and were added to. It's interesting to note that Europe's first true absolute monarch, Louis XIV of France (r. 1643–1715), also put into place rules that required his more powerful nobles to live "with" him at his palace at Versailles. He did so for the same reasons that Iemitsu did and achieved the same results.

Many historians believe that by the time of Iemitsu's death in 1651, Japan had become a forerunner of the totalitarian states of the 20th century.

Illustration 3: Tokugawa clan mon (crest).

Chapter 2 – The Prelude to the Meiji Era

Many Japanese histories and many Japanese themselves state that the imperial family of Japan has ruled or reigned over the "Land of the Rising Sun" for two thousand years or more. Legend has it that the fabled emperor Jimmu Tenno ("Tenno" meaning "Heavenly Sovereign") arrived in Japan with his people (likely from mainland Asia) in 660 BCE. This is purely legend, and the twenty-eight emperors before the first verified emperor in 500 CE likely are as well, as some of them were purported to have lived hundreds of years.

Before the 20th century, specifically the latter half of it (after WWII changed everything), the vast majority of Japanese believed that the legend of Jimmu Tenno was absolutely true. Even today, far-right Japanese nationalists will argue that Jimmu Tenno actually existed and will not brook any disagreement.

What is true is that the Japanese imperial family, up to the moment of this writing, is the longest-reigning monarchy in history. What's more, for most of that time, the monarch and his family were considered divine. They were gods on Earth descended from the sun goddess Amaterasu (still venerated in the native Japanese religion of Shintoism), and they reigned in an unbroken line. Once again, conservative and far-right Japanese still hold this belief today, though, at the end of WWII, the Japanese were forced by the

United States and its military governor in Japan, General Douglas MacArthur, to create a new constitution that clearly rejected the notion of imperial divinity. The vast majority of Japanese today recognize that the emperor is an important figurehead, a symbol of continuity and the state, but most scoff at the notion that the emperor is divine.

From the late 500s to 1192, the imperial family ruled the country, sometimes directly and sometimes, especially in the case of a weak or uninterested monarch, through others. For centuries, the Hojo clan held the most important and powerful offices in the imperial household. However, in 1192, a powerful samurai named Minamoto Yoritomo (remember, the last or family name is first in Japanese culture) established the first shogunate and ruled in the emperor's name. With little interruption, this system of sidelining the emperor and ruling in his stead lasted until the end of the Tokugawa bakufu in 1868.

The decline of Tokugawa rule in Japan began in the 1700s, but one likely did not recognize it at the time. The shogun ruled absolutely, and the daimyo and their samurai, which made up perhaps 3 to 5 percent of the population at most, enforced the laws and customs of Japan ruthlessly.

Everyone knew their place, and for those at the very bottom, their place did not even allow them to choose their own name, at least in official records. A person was known by what one did. You were "farmer" or "blacksmith." Now, of course, in records, you might be "Blacksmith who lives in such and such village on this road or that," but to your neighbors, you might be the Japanese equivalent of "Joe" or "Sam." You would never answer a samurai who asked your name with anything other than "Blacksmith," though. Japan had a place for everyone, and no one deviated from their place.

It is not a Hollywood exaggeration to say that a samurai, even the lowliest, had the right to kill a peasant at any time, for any reason. Did they? Of course not. An unjustified killing would possibly bring disorder, revolt, or, at the very least, economic chaos in a small village. Still, the samurai ruled absolutely. They knew it, flaunted it, and enjoyed it.

However, their enjoyment is one of the reasons the samurai and the military-style order of things broke down. The essential purpose of warriors is to make war. Under the Tokugawa and the policy of Sakoku, life was strictly regimented to prevent revolts (though they did happen sporadically throughout the Tokugawa era and before) and limited foreign contact to the islands in Nagasaki Bay.

In 1800, out of a population of 30 million, there were about 900,000 samurai. Warriors who studied war and the martial arts as their primary duty had no wars to fight, at least for most of the Tokugawa era. That was two hundred years with no major conflicts. By the end of the Tokugawa regime, many samurai could not even use a sword with any real efficiency, and virtually none had ever drawn blood. This meant a number of things. When the foreigners did come back, the samurai were unable to defend their country (of course, the foreigners had modern weapons as well). Secondly, peasant revolts during times of famine and injustice were more difficult to put down.

Since there were no wars, many samurai became restless and yearned for a time when they could do what they were meant to do—fight. Other samurai, whose incomes and privileges were guaranteed by the bakufu, became idle. Some became accomplished writers, while others simply became "idlers," whiling away their time drinking, gambling, and going to the famous Japanese dramas (mostly kabuki, which was considered somewhat "common," but they also attended Noh plays—sort of a Shakespearian-level theater enjoyed by the elite of the elite— and kyogen comedies.

For those who could afford it and even for those who could not and were willing to go into debt, the ultimate pastimes were in the "Floating World" (sometimes translated as "transient" or "fleeting" world), *Ukiyo*. You might be familiar with this term from the art genre of the time (and its offshoots today) known as *Ukiyo-e*, or "portraits of the Floating World."

In Edo, in particular, there was a section devoted to nothing but the senses and pleasure. Back in the 19th century, Edo was the most populous city on Earth, with approximately one million people living within it in 1800. The "Floating World" was situated in the Yoshiwara district and had been since the rise of the Tokugawa in the 1600s. For much of its existence, the *Ukiyo* of Yoshiwara was considered somewhat respectable, but by the time the Tokugawa bakufu ended, it had become somewhat seedy. Most of its denizens were criminals or at least corrupt.

Unless one was a very-high ranking samurai or, in the 19th century, a member of the rising and wealthy Edo middle class and could have a geisha or courtesan sent to you, one would go to *Ukiyo*. There, people could find female companionship, as well as gambling, drinking, gossip, and theater.

Though the culture of old Japan has become relatively well known in the West through books and movies such as *Shogun, The Last Samurai,* and *Memoirs of a Geisha,* it's important to understand that, at least by definition and for most of the life of the "Floating World," a geisha and a courtesan were two entirely different things. Within each group, there were different levels, skills, and, of course, prices.

Courtesan, as you might already know, is a more polite synonym for prostitute. However, the courtesans of the Floating World were not street-walkers, though recent studies have recently delved into the history of courtesans in Japan and the Floating World. They discovered that life, even for the most celebrated, beautiful, and skilled courtesans, was one of sheer sexual slavery. While those in the upper tier who "entertained" the more powerful and wealthy had a better life and could possibly buy out their contracts, they were forced to have sex with men they did not know or even like. This held true even for those who were in high demand. While they might refuse a low-ranking samurai or rude middle-class merchant, there was always a point at which a woman was forced to engage in sex with someone not truly of her own choosing. For those just starting out (perhaps a pretty girl from the provinces sent to make money to send home to her family), there was no choice. Girls as young as twelve were "introduced" to this life for much of its existence.

A courtesan's price would start to go down as she grew older. She might be "fortunate" enough to become the *mama-san* of a house, which she would rule with an iron fist. Others not so fortunate would simply be turned out on the street or perhaps become cooks or do some other menial tasks, either in the Floating

World or elsewhere.

Illustration 4: An entire style of art, Ukiyo-e ("portraits of the Floating World"), grew up around the pleasure areas of Japan. This is an example by the 19th-century master Hiroshige.
Creative Commons CCO, https://publicdomainreview.org/collection/utagawa-hiroshige-last-great-master-of-ukiyo-e

For centuries, one of Japan's cultural icons has been the geisha (which is both a singular and plural noun). Unfortunately, there has also been much misunderstanding surrounding the role of the geisha ever since Japan opened to the world in the mid-19th century. A geisha is not a courtesan or a prostitute, though, toward the end of the Tokugawa era, when corruption and poverty were rife, many geisha did become involved in the "trade." Conversely, many courtesans and prostitutes also tried to pass themselves off as geisha, although usually not well.

An actual geisha underwent long years of training. They would begin at a young age, with training lasting into her late teens and early twenties. This training had nothing to do with actual sex or even, in most cases, physical contact. A geisha, especially one in Edo and one working (and living) in one of the more expensive geisha houses, was expected to be well-versed in music and poetry and conversant and knowledgeable on a wide variety of subjects. (Even though many geisha were aware of the political and social happenings of the time, generally speaking, they did not engage their clients in talk or gossip of this kind.) She was to be the epitome of manners and of Japanese femininity. She had to practice every possible movement of dance and the innumerably enticing and exciting ways a woman might move. She was not a waitress, but she would, depending on the client and perhaps his pocketbook, feed him at meals served by others. Perhaps the most important ritual for a geisha to master was the famous Japanese tea ceremony, an intricately subtle ritual fraught with great meaning.

Perhaps the most famous aspect of the geisha is their appearance. You have likely seen pictures of geisha, or at least women made up to look like geisha. If a woman was successful, she might be able to accumulate a collection of fantastic kimonos (the famous Japanese robe that comes in a variety of styles and colors; there were unwritten but well-known rules for wearing the kimono at certain times of the year, certain events, etc.). In the truest form, the geisha was to resemble and remind a client of a being from another world—in this case, the Floating World—and her gait and manner of movement were deliberately meant to give the impression that she was almost floating above the ground.

Illustration 5: Restored early 20ᵗʰ-century photo of three geisha.
https://www.goodfreephotos.com/japan/other-japan/group-of-geishas.jpg.php

Though geisha still exist today, it seems to be a dying art. While one can visit a geisha house as a tourist today or hire one for a specific occasion, unless you have very good or wealthy business connections in Japan, the geisha you hire is likely to be an amateur. Any Japanese could spot it. The few true remaining geisha houses cater mostly to big corporations for important events, visiting dignitaries, and politicians. Wealth will also buy you a classic experience.

One of the more curious aspects of Japanese culture today, at least to those on the outside looking in, is hostess bars. These places, which run from seedy to exclusive, hire foreign women (almost exclusively Caucasian women from Europe or North America) to entertain Japanese businessmen. To be quite honest, some of the women do extend "extra services" to a client, but most do not. The hostess bar is actually a continuation of the geisha experience, with some major changes and cultural differences, though what the Japanese are paying for is mostly conversation that they cannot or will not have with their wives for a variety of reasons. Some hostesses can make six-figure incomes when converted to US dollars.

An oft-overlooked aspect of the Floating World was its self-governing nature. Though it was overseen by the government bureaucracy, the denizens of *Ukiyo* and their activities were considered somewhat shady and involved dealing with money and bookkeeping, something the samurai had traditionally looked down upon. To that end, if taxes were paid, the pleasure palaces of *Ukiyo* were generally left to run themselves. Unfortunately, as the government weakened and corruption became rife, the *Ukiyo* were run more and more by organized criminal gangs. Price, quality, honesty, and cleanliness went downhill.

Though a middle class of non-samurai was developing in Japan prior to the mid-1800s when the nation was opened to the world, it grew exponentially after the arrival of new technologies brought in from the outside world. The rising middle class began to "take over" the world of *Ukiyo* since they could afford it. Most samurai could not; they had been on a strictly regulated income for centuries. In the world of *Ukiyo*, the middle class flaunted their newfound riches and power, and the samurai began to realize that perhaps their time had come. This caused jealousy and, more importantly, a great deal of resentment in the traditional upper class.

"Dutch Learning"

There were many reasons for the immense changes that happened in and to Japan in the second half of the 1800s. One was an increasingly remote (and many times inept and uninterested) shogun. Many monarchies in history have shown the same general pattern: powerful and dynamic founders, followed by one or two good (or at least efficient) rulers, followed by power-hungry but inept heirs. At some point, a reformer or conscientious ruler will bring new life to a kingdom or empire, but despite its outward appearance, the nation was usually in a period of decline. The dynasty would typically end through a palace coup or revolt of some type or other.

This was the situation in Japan in 1853. Though the policy of isolation was still in effect, it was much easier to prevent people from entering and leaving their assigned trading posts in Japan's far south than it was to stop their ideas. Under Iemitsu and the next few shogun, contact with foreigners was strictly limited. But as the 18th century passed into the 19th century, lax leadership led to law-breaking (in the form of contact during smuggling), carefully guarded acquaintanceships, or even, in a few rare cases, real friendships with Westerners. Knowledge and ideas from the Western world came to Japan.

The vast majority of the foreigners arriving in Nagasaki were Dutch. Though Japan was opened to all Europeans in the 1850s, all Western learning entering Japan, no matter where the Westerners might be from, was called "Dutch learning."

Philipp Franz von Siebold was a Bavarian who first traveled on a Dutch ship to Nagasaki in 1823 as a member of a trade mission for the Dutch East India Company. Siebold was an extremely learned man and had signed onto a Dutch vessel as a medical officer and surgeon in order to have the opportunity to visit the Dutch colony located in today's nation of Indonesia. He stayed in the Dutch East Indies for a year, continuing both his medical practice and studying the local flora. Siebold, like many doctors of the time, was an accomplished botanist. When the opportunity to travel to Japan arose, Siebold took it and spent the next eight years on the island of Deshima, to which the Dutch (and the Chinese) had been assigned.

Deshima was not completely isolated. It was a relatively large port for Dutch and Chinese ships. By the 1800s, when Siebold lived there, Deshima was a developed crescent-shaped complex of living quarters, warehouses, and shops separated from Nagasaki by the length of a gang-plank or small bridge.

When Siebold's knowledge of medicine became known in Edo, permission was given for Japanese doctors to cross into Deshima to speak with and learn from the German doctor. As his reputation spread, Siebold was permitted to begin a medical school in Nagasaki. Though many people will say that Dutch is a particularly difficult language to use (and for Japanese to pronounce), it became the language of the medical school. In addition to learning a Western language, the fifty or so Japanese students who could fit into the building at any one time learned about the science of vaccination, which soon spread throughout the country, saving many Japanese lives. They also learned about human anatomy.

Though the Japanese did have knowledge of the basic structure and interior of the body, the idea of examining the organs and brain of a dead person (or animal) was abhorrent to most Japanese for religious and spiritual reasons. Dead bodies, which had no spirit, represented disease and decay. But with exposure to Siebold's lessons and the realization that much could be learned from an up-close-and-personal study of anatomy, Japanese medical students took up the practice of dissection eagerly.

Though Western medical knowledge in the 19th century was quite rudimentary compared to today, it was, quite literally, two hundred years ahead of the Japanese. Soon, Dutch medical books, references, and anatomical drawings were circulating in Japan, and many were translated into Japanese. As it had in 17th-century Europe, dissection and the development of the scientific method in Japan, especially in regard to medicine, fundamentally changed the Japanese view of the human body and its many functions.

During his stay in Japan (1823–1831), Siebold lived with a Japanese woman and had a daughter with her. Both remained in Japan after the German doctor returned home to become a noted "expert" on Japan (despite only being exposed to a small, educated, and limited portion of Japanese society). Siebold's Japanese "wife," Kusumoto Taki, gave birth to a daughter, Kusumoto Ine, who became the first Japanese woman to become a doctor in Japan. She became the obstetrician for one of the emperor's concubines and later taught obstetrics.

Siebold's teachings opened the floodgates, as the Japanese quickly realized they were centuries behind the West in many ways. They began to devour any and all *Rangaku* ("Dutch learning," though the term came to mean knowledge from any Western nation) they could lay their hands on. In addition to medicine, *Rangaku* included essays, books, and diagrams stemming from the ongoing Industrial Revolution in Europe. They also learned about astronomy, the stock market, other business practices, and much else. As you can imagine, this slowly began to lead to some changes in Japanese life, especially in the cities of Nagasaki and Edo.

For the bakufu, *Rangaku* led many Japanese to an important conclusion: their system of government, their isolation, and their class system were holding them back. Within the regime, officials began to realize that the West was far more advanced, particularly in terms of military strength. Unfortunately for the regime, conservative elements within it, starting with the shogun (who, in 1823 when Siebold arrived, was Tokugawa Ienari, the longest-ruling shogun of the Tokugawa clan, ruling from 1787 to 1837), decided that rather than embrace the new knowledge, he would attempt to purge Japan of it, passing laws forbidding its sale or distribution. While this did limit the spread of "Dutch learning," it did not stop it completely. Still, in 1853, when strange black clouds were seen on the horizon of Edo Bay, the Japanese were unprepared for what was coming to their shores.

Chapter 3 – The Meiji Restoration

Illustration 6: Commodore Matthew C. Perry

Mathew Benjamin Brady, https://commons.wikimedia.org/w/index.php?curid=11076907

The arrival of American warships in Edo Bay on July 8th, 1853, was like one of the many earthquakes that Japan has experienced throughout its lifetime, except, at least figuratively, the four American steamships' effects under the command were much longer-lasting than any mere earthquake, no matter how big. Commodore Matthew Perry's arrival changed Japan forever, and what's more, everyone who witnessed it and read about it knew that it was going to—they just could not predict how.

Perry was a very experienced shipbuilder, and his rank of commodore (to which he was appointed in 1840 as commandant of the New York Naval Shipyard) was unique. Until 1857, there had been no rank higher than that of captain in the US Navy. Perry was one of the most experienced commanders in the US Navy, having joined at the age of fifteen in 1809. His long career saw him take part in many campaigns, including the War of 1812 and the Mexican-American War. Perry is known as the "Father of the Steam Navy" for his advocacy of the newest technology of the time— steam power—which would allow vessels to travel the globe without worrying about finding themselves stranded in the middle of the ocean without wind, which could sometimes take weeks and, at times, was deadly. Steam power also allowed for the storage of coal in areas around the world, which gave all steam-powered navies increased range and speed.

The Japanese did not have a navy or at least one that we (or Perry) would recognize. There were larger coastal vessels for fishing and perhaps pursuing pirates in coastal waters, but the Japanese did not have the capability, desire, or even permission to voyage to other lands.

What's more, any Japanese firearms were patterned on firearms they had obtained in the 1600s from the Portuguese and early Dutch visitors. Firearms were strictly controlled. A daimyo might have some units with firearms, but an overabundance of them would gain the attention of the bakufu. What few cannons that existed were originals from the 1600s or poor copies that either did not function or were more of a danger to their crew than to the enemy.

By contrast, the US naval ships that arrived in Edo were armed with the latest cannons. They had a range far beyond anything of which the Japanese could even conceive. Making matters worse for the Japanese was the fact that Perry's cannons fired a new type of shell that exploded and sprayed shrapnel. For a country where the vast majority of buildings were constructed of wood, this was a very dangerous weapon.

The sailors aboard Perry's ships carried rifled muskets, which fired the most recent technology in firearms, the Minié ball, which resembles today's bullets. Both the rifling (the grooves within the barrel that spin a projectile, making a weapon more accurate over a longer distance) and the Minié ball allowed the Americans to fire more rapidly and at a greater range than the famed samurai archers.

In the 1800s, there had been occasional attempts by Western powers to open Japan, mainly for the purposes of trade. These were attempted through diplomatic notes and negotiations by foreign ships arriving at Deshima/Nagasaki. In 1842, the Dutch king sent a message to the shogun, respectfully explaining that the world had changed since the 1600s and that Japan would be completely outmatched militarily if they should fire upon European ships with their old-fashioned cannons. Still, all of these European attempts were rebuffed, with the Japanese refusing to allow the Europeans to land (including the Russians in the north). Until Perry, no Western power had thought to simply *ignore* Japan's demands.

Perry arrived off the coast of Edo, the de facto Japanese capital. This was no accident. Perry was determined to open Japan to US trade, and he knew that an arrival in Nagasaki would not only be rebuffed but also be seen as being obeisant to the Japanese, something Perry and the Americans were definitely not going to be. Coming to Nagasaki would also give the bakufu the impression that the Americans were going to take the same tack as other foreigners who had visited the country before. Perry's whole plan involved making an undeniable impression on the Japanese.

To that end, when he arrived and was greeted by a contingent of Japanese, he presented them with two things: a white flag and a letter that stated the Americans would open fire on the Japanese coast if they did not allow him to give a letter (written in Dutch) from the United States to the shogun. He had also accompanied his arrival with a volley of blanks from the seventy-three cannons on his flagship, the *Susquehanna*. Perry told the Japanese delegation that this was a celebration of the Fourth of July (America's day of independence), but everyone recognized the volley for what it truly was: a message. Perry's ship alone outgunned all of Japan, and he had brought a whole fleet.

The Japanese official in charge of communicating with the newcomers was Abe Masahiro, and he found himself between a rock and a hard place. If he allowed the Americans to come ashore, he would likely be put to death. If he refused the American commodore, Perry would likely open fire on the nearby village of Uraga. Abe Masahiro stalled for three days, telling the American that he had to wait for instructions. Masahiro decided that accepting the American's letter would be a safe course of action. Perry then told the Japanese of his intention to return to Japan in one year's time. If the Japanese government was not willing to open their country by then, he would.

In actuality, Masahiro had sent back to Edo for instructions, but the shogun, Tokugawa Ieyoshi, was ill and died of heart failure shortly after Perry's departure. Because of this, the Japanese bureaucracy's inaction (they were likely waiting out the illness of the shogun and the possible ascent of his heir), and the novel nature of the problem posed by the Americans' arrival, the Japanese could not take any action before Perry left. This was made much worse when the new shogun, Tokugawa Iesada, and his court did the unthinkable: they asked the daimyo of Japan for advice. Though the shogunate had been weakening for some time, it never (at least not openly and never to more than one or two trusted vassals) asked advice. It ruled, and it needed to be seen as both decisive and dynamic. When word spread that the shogunate had asked the opinion of many of the leading daimyo, most literate Japanese knew that a radical change was likely coming.

Illustration 7: Perry's return in 1854. The armed sailors came ashore, and gun salutes were offered to "honor" the Japanese.

https://en.wikipedia.org/wiki/File:Commodore-Perry-Visit-Kanagawa-1854.jpg

Perry returned three months early with more ships. Upon his arrival, it was made clear that the Japanese were willing to negotiate the opening of their country and the establishment of diplomatic relations with the United States. As you read above, the American's intention was made quite clear to the Japanese—resistance was futile. To a large degree, this was true, and since the Japanese were in a distinctly weak position, they signed the first of what is known to history as the "unequal treaties." The US and Japan signed the Treaty of Kanagawa on March 31st, 1854, which opened two ports to the United States and established an American diplomatic presence in the small city of Shimoda, not far south of Edo, which opened in 1856. Word soon traveled the diplomatic corridors of Europe, and within a year or two, Great Britain, France, Russia, and Japan's old friend Holland had signed similar treaties.

In the 1840s, the Chinese had lost the two Opium Wars to Great Britain, a military defeat that greatly shocked the Chinese. As a result, they were forced to cede some territory and sign economically disadvantageous treaties. Japan knew of this, and in the late 1850s, the Japanese did their best to avoid the same fate.

They did not want their country taken from them piece by piece.

Though Japan had been cornered and forced to sign the unequal treaties with a not-so-subtle threat of force, it did not lose any battles to the Westerners. No Westerners had been killed, so tempers were a bit cooler when it came to Japan compared to China. The Japanese knew a major conflict would be incredibly costly in terms of both lives and treasure and would likely end with a much worse treaty being forced upon them.

The unequal treaties gave the Western nations some decided advantages. They controlled the amount of the Japanese tariff, became established in many Japanese coastal cities, and enjoyed the benefits of "extra-territoriality" (meaning Westerners breaking the law in Japan would be tried in Western courts, not Japanese courts). However, while they included provisions and the understanding that Japan (to paraphrase) "was not equal to the West" (meaning it was not modern or industrialized and did not have a modern constitution), Japan would be treated equally when it did modernize. The West was more than happy to help the Japanese do that for a price: unequal trade and riches, which it did receive.

Ironically for the Western powers, they got what they asked for. In forty years, Japan had become a modernized nation, faster than any nation in history. Only perhaps China, from 1990 to 2020, has replicated the feat, but transportation and technology were much different in 1860, making Japan's transformation even more impressive.

Perry's visit had another impact. While the Japanese had been governed by one regime since 1603, the island was still fragmented. In their everyday lives, most Japanese, including the samurai, had not left their own provinces. The bi-annual trip to Edo as "guests" of the shogunate did not count, as it was not a tourist trip. What's more, the only real "government" most Japanese dealt with on an everyday basis was that of their local lord. So, while most Japanese knew that their compatriots in other parts of the islands were Japanese, the country and culture were not truly united.

This was similar to the situation in the United States before the Civil War. Before the conflict, most Americans did not identify as such. They considered themselves to be from their individual states, though they knew they were in a union with the others. They were

Pennsylvanians or Virginians. After the Civil War, Americans began to call themselves that, though that took a bit longer in the South.

This is what began to happen in Japan after the imposition of the unequal treaties. While the humiliation was great to many in the bakufu, for many Japanese, this feeling of national humiliation was both slow in coming and spurred great strides.

History is strange, and fate can turn on a dime, which is essentially what happened when Perry showed up at Japan's doorstep with his "black ships." The Japanese could understand military force, and they knew what cannons were, but one episode might have impressed the Japanese more than the cannons. As part of the "diplomatic niceties" of Perry's second visit, a small cultural event was conducted. The Japanese held a sumo wrestling match for the Americans. It was likely meant to both entertain and send a message of Japanese strength to the foreigners. The Americans found the large, adipose, very non-athletic-appearing wrestlers to be quite funny—and not in a good way.

Commodore Perry was known to be an absolute fanatic about railroads and steam trains, and he brought a 1/25th-scale model of a steam engine and 100 meters of railroad tracks with him to Japan. People could ride aboard, and many of the important Japanese present did so. When the train was given to them as a gift, it was taken back to Edo and studied *very* carefully. Modern technology had arrived in Japan.

The Samurai in Decline

However, before the unique Japanese "Industrial Revolution" took place, other changes had to occur, although, to a large extent, they had already been occurring. The samurai were warriors without war. Many spent their time in idle pleasures, going into debt and sinking many times into drunkenness. The last time the samurai had any sort of glory was back in the early 1700s when the famous forty-seven ronin ("master-less samurai") avenged their lord's death and committed seppuku. That story has been fictionalized and made into plays, movies, artwork, and more. Today, it is almost as popular in Japan as it was in the 18th century. It displays the samurai ideals of bravery, service, and loyalty unto death and has come to make up a part of the Japanese psyche, especially in the mid-1900s.

However, by the time Perry had arrived, the samurai had not only lost their sense of purpose but also, in many ways, their privileged status. Though the middle class in Japan would explode in the later 1800s, by the time of the unequal treaties, trading houses and banks in Japan had created a small and extremely wealthy middle class of merchants, who were officially almost at the bottom of the Japanese class system. They did not keep order, they didn't grow food, and many Japanese, especially the samurai, despised them. However, with the arrival of foreigners and the increasing importance of trade and manufacturing, the samurai lost their place of prestige. Many went into debt. A growing feeling among non-samurai was that the warrior class had become parasites. They could not defend Japan from the outside world and did virtually nothing for their income, lands, and power.

For the Westerners, Japan presented a different situation than what they had faced in China, India, Africa, and South America. In those places, factionalism and disorder made it easier for Westerners to move in. However, it also made those places more difficult to trade with—especially when compared to Japan.

In the 1850s and 1860s, Japan was an orderly, clean, polite society with a long-established government that had the administrative capabilities to oversee effective trade and negotiate with foreigners. Most Westerners who visited Japan on trade or diplomatic missions (there were a few ultra-wealthy tourists who wanted to visit the unique islands of Japan) were enthralled by the Japanese and their culture. The Japanese were exceedingly polite but so culturally different; it almost seemed as if they were from another planet. Japanese art, porcelain, lacquer-ware, kimonos, fans, and much else (including very explicit sex manuals that became the secret rage in Victorian England) were immensely popular. Those who could establish ties with Japanese porcelain makers became very rich importers back home in Europe and the US.

Japan was backward, at least economically and technologically, which was evident even to the Japanese. What was equally obvious was that the bakufu had to go. There had been peasant rebellions in the 18th and early 19th centuries, and they were put down ruthlessly. But each revolt had gotten larger and became more and more difficult to put down. Eventually, to the anger of many samurai, the peasants were given more rights, including reforms over landownership and taxation.

Many samurai were also angered over the ease at which the foreigners had "invaded" Japan. Many of these samurai came from the south of the country, which was governed a bit less strictly than the domains closer to Edo. The daimyo in the south resented the growing presence of the foreigners, their ideas, and the changes that were coming to the country. Model trains were not the only things that came to Japan. Western-style factories were being built with foreign help and money. The samurai and their way of life, which they considered the "real" Japanese way of life, was ending.

Some of these samurai were sent to the US, Great Britain, Germany, and elsewhere to learn about economics, politics, technology, farming, and much else. Many of these diplomats, which began to include wealthy and educated non-samurai by the 1870s, were enamored by what they saw. The most immediate and visible effect of these visits became the unbelievable popularity of Western-style clothing in Japan from the 1870s onward.

The Japanese craze for Western clothing continued into the 1920s and 1930s, especially some of the "racier" women's fashions. With the advent of the military dictatorship in the early 1930s, this was discouraged.

The craze for clothing was not a one-way street. Japanese-style clothes were exported to Europe and the US, and visitors to Japan often went to the new Japanese photo studios to have a souvenir picture taken in Japanese clothing.

Illustration 8: The Conte di Bardi in Japan, late 1800s.
https://commons.wikimedia.org/wiki/File:Conte_di_Bardi.jpg

The Fall of the Bakufu

The fuse to the very large powder keg that sat underneath the bakufu had been laid a long time before the foreigners arrived. Tokugawa Iesada's age and poor health when the Americans arrived did not help matters. Iesada died in 1858. His successor, Iemochi, came to power in 1858 at the age of twenty-two. He reigned for eight years, proving to be a weak and inefficient ruler.

In 1862, Iemochi married the emperor's daughter to strengthen the bakufu. This was the *kobu gattai* movement ("the Union of Court and Bakufu"), which would hopefully give added strength to the shogun and increase his influence. However, this did not happen. Other developments had made this attempt a tardy (and desperate) one.

By the end of Iemochi's reign, the shogunate was under pressure from many sides. There were the foreigners, whose influence in Japan was growing. They were also struggling with each other, at least diplomatically and economically, for influence and riches in Japan.

Then there were the daimyo and samurai known as the *shishi* or "men of purpose," whose goal was to restore the emperor and his direct rule. These men believed that the Tokugawa shogunate was illegitimate and had usurped the rightful power of the imperial court. The rallying cry of this movement was "sonno joi" ("revere the emperor and repel the barbarians"). Like other cultures around the world, many Japanese, even those who welcomed the foreigners, believed them to be barbarians. The Westerners had different, uncouth, and disgusting habits like eating meat (which soon became a staple in Japan despite the nation's initial revulsion). The Westerners also had a pronounced aversion to bathing. In a turnabout situation, foreigners living in Japan soon came to appreciate the relaxing, social, and health benefits of regular bathing! Even today, Japanese and their still somewhat insular culture will refer to foreigners as *gaijin*, which can mean "outsider" or "alien" and has differing connotations determined by context and tone.

One of the interesting facets of some of the *shishi* was their pragmatic view of the "barbarians." In the majority of cases, the desire to expel the *gaijin* was not based on racial hatred to any real degree; rather, it was a revulsion toward some of their manners and appearance because they were new. The desire to rid Japan of foreigners was based on the idea that the Westerners were changing Japan's unique culture into one just like their own. Additionally, many *shishi* and non-samurai were worried that the Western powers would soon divide Japan up into colonies or dependencies. In other words, Japan would lose its independence.

The third group was the *tozama daimyo*. These were the descendants of the daimyo who had fought Tokugawa Ieyasu and his bid to rule all of Japan. Those daimyo, for the most part, were from the southern part of Japan or had been forcefully located there to be isolated from the center of power. They had been allowed to retain most of their rights but were viewed with suspicion, even two hundred years later. In addition, the *tozama daimyo* had the closest contact with foreigners throughout the period of isolation. A small number of Japanese, including samurai, were still Christian as well. The bakufu suspected many of the southern lords as being Christian, even when they were not. To the bakufu, being Christian meant that a person's loyalty lay with a foreign god and/or church and not the shogun and, through him, the emperor.

The *tozama daimyo*, especially the rival (and powerful) southern daimyo of Choshu and Satsuma, were growing restive with the bakufu's incompetence, not only in the case of the foreigners but also in their governance of the islands. Corruption was especially a problem. Many of the young *shishi* were centered in *tozama* lands, making matters more complicated. While the *tozama* lords were "anti-foreign" (at least to the point of believing the foreigners needed to be reined in and watched), they also believed there was much to be learned from them. This caused a certain level of conflict in the *tozama* domains but not enough to deter them from their goal.

The two most powerful *tozama daimyo*, those of Choshu and Satsuma, had long been rivals. They had struggled with each other for influence with the shogunate. By the 1860s, their contact with foreign powers had gotten them early access and a head start on the purchase of weapons and their development. Additionally, the populations of the *tozama* domains were close to 25 percent samurai, which was much higher than in other domains, especially where lands were more amenable to farming. Though the samurai of the 1800s were different from those of the late 1500s and early 1600s, most samurai spent much of their time training in various martial arts, including the use of firearms. Worse still, for the bakufu, the Choshu samurai were doing something revolutionary—arming non-samurai. By the second half of the 1860s, the armies of the *tozama daimyo* were larger and more powerful than those of the bakufu, though the shogunate did not know that yet.

In 1864, an uprising was led by the Choshu against the shogunate in the imperial city of Kyoto. The conflict (known as the First Choshu Expedition) between the Choshu and the bakufu ended with an agreement brokered by the Satsuma clan, which was beginning to realize that the bakufu was counting on eliminating the power of the Choshu before coming for them. Therefore, in 1866, the Satsuma and Choshu clans set aside their differences and secretly agreed to an alliance with the ultimate goal of overthrowing the shogunate and restoring the emperor to his proper place. This agreement was brokered by a famous low-ranking but brilliant and influential samurai named Sakamoto Ryoma, who is still the subject of Japanese movies and television today. Aside from the famous Saigo Takamori, the leader of the Satsuma, another famous samurai from this period was Takasugi Shinsaku of Choshu, who was instrumental in the secret efforts to modernize the armies of Satsuma and Choshu.

At about the same time the two *tozama* clans were making their secret alliance, the new shogun, Tokugawa Yoshinobu, decided that the actions taken by the lord of Choshu needed to be addressed. What Yoshinobu did not realize was that the age-old strategy of divide and conquer was not going to work for him. For two centuries, the shogunate had counted on personal feuds and real political differences to keep the Satsuma and Choshu lords separate and loyal, but they had allied themselves. When the shogun called on Satsuma for support against the Choshu, the call fell on deaf ears.

The Tokugawa shogunate was joined by a number of units from smaller provinces and weaker daimyo, not all of whom had a desire to fight or truly supported the shogunate. After an embarrassing defeat in the south, the shogun's forces retreated northward to Edo. A ceasefire was agreed upon in the summer of 1866, and though the shogunate made a number of compromises that allowed power to be decentralized, virtually everyone in Japan knew that the bakufu's days were numbered.

Oddly enough, however, the emperor of the time, Komei, was more inclined to support the shogun and his increasingly anti-foreign stance rather than rule himself. There was also a concern that Japan might find itself in the midst of a destructive civil war.

In 1867, a new conflict broke out between the *tozama daimyo* (now joined by an increasing number of less powerful daimyo and samurai) and the Tokugawa shogun. This was the Boshin War (named for a period on the Japanese calendar of the time). The war ended with the defeat of Tokugawa Yoshinobu at the Battle of

Hakodate on the northern island of Hokkaido, far from Edo, which itself had seen a popular uprising against the Tokugawa. Eventually, the Tokugawa established a weak domain on Hokkaido known as the Republic of Ezo, but this, too, was defeated. One of the powerful leaders of the rebellion, Saigo Takamori, was advised by the Western powers that killing the shogun would have an adverse effect on relations. He allowed Yoshinobu to retire in peace, though he remained under close surveillance. He died in 1912.

The stated goal of the rebellion was to restore the emperor to power after centuries of ruling shoguns, generals, and daimyo ruling in his name. Fortunately for the *sonno joi* movement, Emperor Komei, who had supported the bakufu, died in 1867. His son, Mutsuhito, became the 122nd emperor of Japan on February 3rd, 1867.

The Meiji Era

Before we continue, we should take a moment to talk about the Japanese emperor and his name. Before the accession of the new emperor in 1867, the reign of an emperor was divided into eras, and era names are the ones used in histories of the Japanese imperial family today. An era (or "reign") name could only be used once, and it only was used after the emperor died. In the case of Emperor Komei, his birth name was Osahito. It was only after his death that he was known as Komei, which has its roots in an archaic naming system that came from China. Osahito's son was named Mutsuhito, but Mutsuhito is known to history as Emperor Meiji, which means "enlightened one" or "enlightened ruler." During his reign (and the reigns of all Japanese emperors), he was simply known as "Emperor" to the public or "His Imperial Highness." No one but close members of the imperial family ever called him Mutsuhito, but that is the name he signed on documents.

Illustration 9: Meiji, 1872, wearing the sokutai garb reserved for the upper strata of the ruling class for very formal occasions.
https://en.wikipedia.org/wiki/File:Meiji_tenno3.jpg

Debate continues today among those who study Japanese history as to what kind of man and ruler Meiji was. Most agree that while he had the final say in policy decisions, he often left those decisions to the men immediately underneath him—the *genro*—an unofficial body of five of the most influential and powerful daimyo, including those from Satsuma and Choshu. We know that Meiji sat in on virtually all of his cabinet meetings and those of his advisers but remained silent for all of them.

Japan and Emperor Meiji were treading new ground. For hundreds of years, commoners rarely even saw the emperor. When he did address groups of people, it was frequently from behind an elaborate screen on a throne. Meiji allowed himself to be photographed and seen in public, which was a first. For instance, he was seen in public when a huge train of retainers, soldiers, important figures, and the imperial household traveled from the ancient imperial capital of Kyoto to the new national capital of Edo, which was renamed Tokyo. It means "capital of the east."

Meiji himself was sickly, though he lived to an older age than the five emperors before him. Meiji suffered from beriberi, a disease that comes from a lack of thiamine (vitamin B-1), which was due to the peculiar diet the imperial family followed. He also suffered from a variety of other illnesses, some of them brought on by genetic defects due to centuries of intermarriage in the imperial family. This practice ended during Hirohito's reign, who was emperor for most of the 20th century. Meiji suffered from mandibular prognathism, which caused a jutting lower jaw, which is common among descendants of intermarriage. Later pictures show him sporting a thick beard to hide this defect. He also had spinal issues, which made it difficult to walk without a cane.

Despite all of these health issues, Meiji managed to have fifteen children with various women. He apparently was not overly fond of either his children or grandchildren, which included two future emperors.

Still, Meiji is associated with the period of the greatest and most rapid changes in the history of Japan and perhaps the world. He is regarded by most Japanese as the "Father of Modern Japan."

For most Japanese, Meiji's ascension and the revolution that had overthrown the Tokugawa shogunate were not regarded as being much different from the rebellions and changes in regimes that had gone on for centuries in Japan. Most of those at the bottom thought their lot would remain the same, and most of those at the top believed they would still enjoy the same privileges they had since time immemorial. To a large degree, both groups were wrong.

On April 7th, 1868, the Charter Oath was put together by the *genro* and their advisers and approved by the emperor. If you think for a moment about what you know about feudal Japan, just from what you've read in this book so far, you'll realize how radical the Charter Oath was. It included the following five pledges:

1) to establish deliberative assemblies in order to involve the public in decision-making;

2) to involve all levels of society "from the highest to the lowest" in state affairs;

3) to abolish restrictions on the occupation and function of all people;

4) to abandon the superstitions of the past and embrace rational laws of nature;

5) to seek knowledge from the outside world to strengthen Japan.

These are radical pledges, and they were followed, although there were some interruptions during the 1930s and 1940s). For the rest of the 19th century, pledges four and five would have the most impact on Japanese policy.

There were two main impetuses to these changes in Japanese policy: to become modern for the sake of the country itself and its ambitions and to be treated as an equal "modern and civilized" nation (those were the words used by both Japanese and Westerners at the time) so Japan could reject the unequal treaties and join the modern world as an equal.

Many in the West believed this would take a very long time, perhaps even a century, though many Westerners who had come to know the Japanese thought the world might be in for a surprise. Those who thought that Japan would lag behind for the foreseeable future did not know the Japanese work ethic, nor did they understand how rapidly technology and information could spread throughout the world by the late 1800s.

The changes in the way Japan was treated by the Western powers (including Russia) came, at least to the Japanese, slowly. Aside from enjoying trade privileges that were not reciprocal, the Westerners were also concerned that their legal rights as individuals, businesses, and nations would not be protected until Japan had a codified, centralized, and Western-style constitution and laws.

The Meiji era was one of unbelievable change and influence. It is hard to overstate the pace of development, especially in a short book such as this. But suffice it to say that, at least regarding the unequal treaties, Japan had completely changed its legal system and achieved "equal" status with the Western powers by the mid-1890s, at least formally. Economic and political treaties were achieved rather fairly, but in the coming years, it seemed (at least to the Japanese) that Japan was still seen as a "backward" country when it came to its military and international affairs.

The Western powers grudgingly began negotiating with Japan as an equal partner. There was great pressure from the Japanese political establishment, which held a slight "ace up their sleeve" in the awarding of contracts to Britain, France, the US, and Germany. The Japanese encouraged competition between them for contracts, especially for weapons (although, at times, the West colluded and pushed the Japanese into a corner). The Japanese public was becoming increasingly well-informed about their nation and the world through a massive education program that allowed universal education through at least grade school and the spread of modern newspapers. (Girls received an education until grade three and were then expected to learn how to keep house and raise children.) Due to the widespread knowledge of the unequal treaties and other news relating to foreigners, the Japanese public put great pressure on both the government and the West with marches, riots, and attacks on foreigners by extremists from both left and right groups.

No, not all Japanese were happy with the changes taking place in the country. The first and foremost of those who had grievances with the government were the samurai, mainly those in the lower ranks. Over time, a large extent of the samurai had become men without purpose, idling their days away in the *Ukiyo* of Tokyo and other large cities, writing poetry and letters, and painting traditional Japanese scenes. Many of them did learn the martial arts, especially kendo—a martial art for swordsmanship using bamboo instead of steel—but they never had the opportunity to use their skills and swords in battle. What action they did see was against the occasional band of robbers and highwaymen.

As the Meiji era continued, most people, especially those of a higher rank, including the daimyo, realized the day of the samurai was over. The Westerners would not stand for a class so distinctly above the others in virtually every way, and neither would the bulk of the Japanese population. Those who were on the bottom had two things in mind: watching the samurai get a taste of karma for the centuries they had total power over the people and getting some of that power for themselves.

Unfortunately for the lower samurai, who held all their lands (if any had not been mortgaged out to the growing middle class to pay debts) at the behest and pleasure of the daimyo, they had virtually no power, even as soldiers. As they saw in the Boshin War, it turned out that modern weapons did not require the same level of practice and training as the "two swords." Plainly put, the samurai were outnumbered and outgunned. The ten thousand samurai who helped the Meiji Restoration take place was soon augmented, and its men were absorbed by the Imperial Japanese Army (IJA), which soon numbered much more than that. The army was made up of conscripts of all classes in 1873. For a number of decades, the officer corps was made up of former samurai or at least men from samurai lineages, but in the 1930s and 1940s, there were far fewer samurai-descended officers, except at the very top.

We say "former samurai" for, within a couple of years, the samurai lost their legal and hereditary privileges. These included the wearing of swords and the traditional samurai top-knot hairstyle. These changes seem small to an outsider, but to a samurai, they were identifiers of his rank and privilege, which had been passed down from his ancestors. More practically, the lower-rank samurai lost the stipends that had been given to them by the government since the start of the Tokugawa regime in 1603. By tradition, samurai disdained the earning and accounting of money. That was done by shopkeepers, who were once seen as almost the lowest of the low. Shopkeepers were looked at as people who produced nothing; they only took the work of others and passed it along.

So, the samurai, who were forbidden by tradition and, at times, the law to work for money, gradually went broke. They made their living by exchanging the rice or other crops grown on their lands. In the modern era, no one wanted to be paid in rice. Not only that, but the amount of rice grown per acre did not grow as fast as inflation, which meant the lower-ranking samurai could not afford to live in the style to which he and his family were accustomed. Their increasing attendance in the brothels, theaters, and gambling halls of the *Ukiyo* did not help either. Soon, the samurai had massive debts. Some sold or leased their lands, though they were not entitled to do so in most cases. Others became criminals. Many wandered the streets drunk, disheveled, and aimless.

Many believe that the samurai lost their self-esteem due to the long period of peace brought on by the Tokugawa shogunate. Traditionally, samurai won or were rewarded with the spoils of war.

This was one reason that Hideyoshi Toyotomi invaded Korea; Japan was at peace, and he needed to pay the samurai for their support. In the latter half of the 19ᵗʰ century, the samurai had lost their purpose, riches, and the esteem of the people, which were supposed to come from their heroism and feats in battle.

For those at the pinnacle of samurai society—the daimyo—things were not as bad. The majority of them were land-rich. Many of them secretly invested in the new manufacturing industries being created in Japan. They leased land to foreigners and the growing number of Japanese manufacturers. The daimyo were also forced to sell all but 10 percent of their hereditary lands. The most powerful daimyo, the five *genro*, sold all of their property and received a generous salary from the new government (of which they were the unofficial head) and appointments as governors of the very same fiefdoms they had ruled as daimyo. This might seem undemocratic, and it surely was, but the new governors consisted of lower-ranking samurai and a number of commoners as well.

The new Japanese government appeared quite democratic, at least on paper. Throughout the 1880s, a movement among the people grew that pressed the new government to pursue what they increasingly saw as their "natural" rights. This movement was greatly influenced by the increasing amounts of Western literature and histories being translated into Japanese and the many Japanese who reported on their experiences in the West after returning from abroad.

The resultant Meiji Constitution of 1889 seemed to be the answer to a great many of the demands of the popular rights movement. It included a legislature with an elected lower house and an appointed upper house (they were appointed by the emperor). It also enumerated a variety of rights and duties.

The Meiji Constitution set the foundation for what was to come after WWII, but power was retained by the emperor, who initially governed through the *genro*. However, as they retired, a similarly powerful cabinet of imperial advisers took their place. The legislature was elected by only about 5 percent of the male population (those in the highest tax bracket) and really only served to advise the emperor and his cabinet.

The Meiji Constitution and local laws created a more equitable court system in which, at least in theory, the poor had the same rights as the rich, and the increasing education of the masses resulted in pressure occasionally being put on the government for change. But in essence, by the mid-1890s, power was held exclusively by those at the top, and that included the military. The slogan of the Japanese government in the Meiji era was "wealthy country, strong military."

Saigo Takamori

The changes happening within Japan were not pleasing to everyone. In 1877, one of the men who had caused the fall of the Tokugawa shogunate and the Meiji Restoration, Saigo Takamori (1828–1877), rebelled against the government for what he saw as weakness. The imperial government was leading Japan astray, as Japan was moving away from its martial glory, which Takamori viewed as its inheritance from the samurai of old.

Interestingly enough, Takamori had been instrumental in assuring the conscription of non-samurai into the army and became one of its top leaders after the Meiji Restoration. During the early part of the Meiji era, when debate raged within Japan about the role of the samurai, Takamori stayed on the sidelines. He apparently did not want to alienate support on either side of the debate. However, he was a militarist. In addition to his ideas about conscription, he (along with another man from a famed samurai family, Yamagata Aritomo) encouraged the modernization of Japan's army and, more importantly, the expansion of Japan into a true empire, one that would eventually rival those of the Western powers.

The most obvious place to begin that overseas empire was Korea, the country closest to Japan and what many samurai had long called a "dagger pointing at the heart of Japan." Takamori and other influential men, both within and outside the government, believed they had the perfect excuse to start a campaign in Korea. The "Hermit Kingdom" (Korea had been known by this name for centuries due to its limited contact with the outside world) had not recognized the new Japanese government under Emperor Meiji. Actually, the Koreans had rebuffed Japanese diplomatic and ambassadorial overtures three times, which would be a serious matter in diplomacy even today. To the Japanese of that era, it was disrespectful to the extreme and required a strong response.

Takamori believed he had the perfect way to provoke a war with the Koreans, one that all of Japan would support. He would go to Korea and insult them in the worst and most provocative ways, forcing them to kill him. This would enrage the Japanese people and government, restore the fighting "samurai spirit" to Japan, and fulfill Takamori's dream of dying for Japan and the emperor. As wild as this sounds, Takamori's idea was initially approved by Meiji in August 1873, but once influential men within the government and the emperor's cabinet heard of the plan, they put a stop to it. They believed war with Korea was foolhardy. It was something that could be done later, but they believed it would provoke a giant response from China and probably Russia. In addition, Japan might expect a poor reaction from the Western powers (France, Germany, Britain, and the United States), which might cause irreparable damage to Japan's progress toward removing the unequal treaties. Takamori was told not to leave Japan.

In response, Takamori resigned from all of his government positions and returned to his home in the city of Kagoshima in Satsuma Province. There, he opened a private school for the physical and martial training of former samurai upset with the changes taking place in Japan. In modern terms, Takamori's school was an extra-legal paramilitary camp. What's more, despite giving up his government positions, Takamori was still one of the most respected and powerful men in the country. Over the next four years, graduates of his school were appointed to positions of responsibility throughout the country, especially in Tokyo.

Throughout 1876, uprisings by former samurai took place in many parts of the country. By 1877, the Japanese government had become more and more alarmed at the growth and influence of Takamori's movement. An estimated twenty thousand students had passed through his school in four years, and no one knew how many others they had influenced. It was time to do something before Takamori destroyed any hope of Japan becoming a "modern" country. However, Takamori made the first move, which saved the government from the trouble of attacking him. On January 29th, 1877, a large group of Takamori's students attacked the government arsenal and shipyard in Kagoshima.

Takamori was not in Kagoshima when this happened and may not have known it was going to, but when he heard of the assault, he returned to Kagoshima. It is said he "reluctantly" agreed to lead a march to Tokyo to present a list of grievances to the government. The government had other ideas, though, and did not wish to be seen tolerating any sort of armed uprising against it, no matter from what quarter. Over the next six months, a battle of attrition and a blockade took place south of Tokyo, which weakened Takamori's smaller and less well-equipped forces. Finally, in late summer, Takamori was forced to retreat back to his home city of Kagoshima with only two hundred followers left out of the forty thousand that had marched toward Tokyo. On September 24th, 1877, the Imperial Japanese Army launched a final attack. Takamori was critically wounded, and he asked his aide to behead him. The Satsuma Rebellion was over, as was the greatest challenge to the modernization of Japan.

Illustration 10: Statue of Takamori in Tokyo today.
https://en.wikipedia.org/wiki/File:SaigoTakamori1332.jpg

Today, Takamori's legacy is a mixed one in Japan. He had made it clear that he was not rebelling against the emperor but rather against many of his advisers. He also cited the changes taking place within Japan; for instance, though the Meiji Constitution called for many somewhat democratic reforms, the government was being run from the top down and was increasingly authoritarian. Takamori also realized that the samurai class needed reform but did not believe it should be eliminated, at least within the military. Still, the emperor did nothing to prevent the final attack that cost Takamori his life, which sent a clear message that the former general who had helped start the Meiji Restoration was considered a rebel of sorts. Even today, Takamori is both reviled and respected by different segments of the Japanese population. Takamori's story was part of the inspiration for the hit 2003 movie *The Last Samurai.*

As the 19th century progressed, many other changes came to Japan. For a relatively short time, Japanese merchants and the few progressive-thinking samurai who did not believe money was beneath them (it was typically seen as the work of women and shopkeepers) began to invest heavily in Western industrial technology. It is hard to imagine today, but quite a few popular movies have been made along the lines of the *Land That Time Forgot*, where a mysterious island is found frozen in a bygone era. This literally was Japan in 1863 and 1864 when Perry made his famous visits. It's also the reason for the length of this chapter. The Meiji era was the foundation of everything that was to come afterward, ending at least 1,500 years of samurai-dominated warrior culture. The changes that happened during the Meiji Restoration are akin to the effects of the American Revolution and the American Civil War on the United States.

Women in Early Modern Japan

Though we will tell you more about the history and lives of women in Japan, it must be admitted that although Japanese women surely played a significant role in the history of Japan, especially behind the scenes, a woman's place was in the home or the fields. In more powerful samurai families, a woman might attend court or become an accomplished artist or writer (many believe Lady Murasaki's *The Tale of Genji*, originally printed circa 1000 CE, was the first true novel). Regardless of class, she would likely be responsible for the arranging of her daughter's marriage. Politics, for the most part, was not a woman's realm, at least not openly or noticeably.

A family's income was managed by the wife. To a great degree, at least in more traditional and rural parts of Japan, this is still the case. This has nothing to do with the men's distaste for money; rather, it is the continuation of a cultural custom. In the age when most Japanese women did not work, it was seen as a way to take pressure off their exhausted husbands.

As you likely know, the traditional form of both men's and women's dress was a loose-fitting robe-like outfit. Today, the most similar outfit worn in Japan is called the *yukata*. It is typically elaborately designed or colored, but it would not have been in the past.

Illustration 11: Farming couple circa 1870s.
https://commons.wikimedia.org/wiki/File:Japanese_peasants._Before_1902.jpg

The most immediate and visible change that took place in the lives of women, at least in Tokyo and the other major cities, was clothing. Kyoto, the former imperial capital, did not "modernize," at least in terms of dress and culture, as quickly as those cities on the coasts that had frequent contact with foreigners. In a male-dominated society such as Japan, the debate over the adoption of Western clothes for men was relatively muted, as a growing number of men were working with, for, or in Western-style businesses and factories. It was considered "modern and civilized" to dress as a Westerner.

Many of the more progressive and Western-looking Japanese men wished their wives or mistresses would be viewed as modern. Japanese women in the cities went crazy for Western fashion after millennia of wearing essentially the same styles (and yes, there are differences, but one needs to have a serious interest in Japanese fashion history to notice most of them). In conservative urban circles, more provincial cities, and rural Japan, Western clothing, at least for women, was looked down upon, though this prejudice was relatively rapidly overcome. Still, the change in dress was symbolic, for more and more women began seeking work in the cities. The adoption of Western-style clothing, with (relatively speaking) a "tighter fit," was also safer than loose garb in the factories.

Industry

The symbol of Japan's growth in the Meiji era was the railroad and the steam train. Commodore Perry's gift of the model train was not simply taken to Edo as an oddity. It showed Japan that the world had truly changed. In 1872, there were less than twenty miles of railroad tracks in Japan. Ten years later, there were nearly 250. In 1887, there were 640. By the end of the 19th century, there were over two thousand miles, and at the outbreak of WWI, Japan had over seven thousand!

With the expansion of railroads, Japan's steel and iron industries grew, as did its coal production. In 1875, the Japanese mined 600,000 tons of coal. In 1913, they mined twenty-one million! However, the growth of the Japanese economy and its need to export to at least try to keep a balance of payments between itself and the West meant that Japanese industry soon outstripped the production of almost all vital commodities, including iron, steel, and coal. In the early 1930s, if not before, Japan was at the mercy of imports. By the late 1930s, the bulk of its iron, coal, and steel imports (as well as its petroleum, which replaced steam power) was arriving from the United States of America.

Japanese production increased by unreal leaps and bounds, but in some areas, production did not simply increase. The machines and even steel were comparable or, in some cases, superior to that of the West by the early 1900s.

Take shipping, for example. To trade with the outside world, the Japanese needed ocean-going steam-powered merchant ships. To protect those ships, at least in the Pacific, Japan needed a modern navy. Of course, that navy would also protect Japan from being humiliated militarily.

In 1893, the naval construction in Japan amounted to an estimated 200,000 to a million and a half tons (recordkeeping, which was traditionally excellent in Japan, was hampered at this time by the rapid changes taking place in the country). In 1913, just before the outbreak of the First World War, Japanese domestic production was over 3.5 million tons, and this does not account for the contracting of warships built in the naval shipyards of other nations, primarily Great Britain, whose naval technology and successes were closely studied and emulated by Japan. Initially, Japan bought older British warships destined for home duty or mothballs (reserve ships), but as Japan became richer, the Japanese designed their own warships to be built in British shipyards. In 1914, some observant British naval officers and shipbuilders noted that the Japanese designs were better than their own.

By the early 1900s, railroad manufacturers and leaders in other industries had come together to make ships, cars, and (eventually) airplanes. You might recognize the names of two of these companies: Mitsubishi and Kawasaki. Others included Mizuno, which now makes sports equipment, as well as Nakajima and Aichi, both of which made warplanes during WWII.

By the latter half of the 1890s, not only had Japan renegotiated the unequal treaties, but she was also ready to embark on a new path. They would embrace imperialism, just like the West.

The First Sino-Japanese War

Korea had long been a target for the Japanese. You saw the results of Hideyoshi's Korean misadventure in the late 1500s and how Saigo Takamori suggested provoking the Koreans as a pretext for Japan to invade.

One must understand that, as wrong as we might see it now, in the second half of the 1800s, the world entered a new period of imperialism. Those at the top of the world's pecking order believed that gaining or enlarging an empire was one of their primary duties.

Japan looked at it the same way. Though the country was evolving into a completely different type of Japan, at least outwardly, no country (especially one in which the warrior class governed without question for a thousand years or more) was going to move enough away from that warrior mentality in just four decades.

The man who was responsible for pioneering the organization and development of the Imperial Japanese Army was also the man who laid the foundation of the Imperial Japanese Navy (IJN): Yamagata Aritomo. When Aritomo began studying the militaries of the West, he believed that two powers were worthy models. At sea, the British were absolutely dominant and had been for over a century. In 1871, the German states had unified around the large Kingdom of Prussia after a series of three wars, which all ended in stunning Prussian victories.

Yamagata Aritomo called Korea part of Japan's "zone of advantage," meaning it was close and had access to even greater powers (Russia and China). If Korea was not controlled by the Japanese, Japan would find itself looking down the barrel of a gun, as a foreign power could easily take Korea and then seek to take Japan next. It would be for the best to move first.

Of course, moving first entailed great risk because China still regarded Korea as a tributary state and part of its sphere of influence. This had been the case for centuries, and in the late 1800s, China was declining in power. Holding on to Korea, especially for reasons of prestige, was paramount for China.

In 1876, a Japanese diplomatic mission, backed by what modern warships the Japanese had at the time, arrived in Korea and threatened action against the Koreans should they not sign what is now known as the Treaty of Kanghwa. Like the Americans had done, the Japanese issued a decree to the Koreans. Korea would not be treated as an equal until it, too, had become "modern and civilized."

Indeed, comparatively speaking, the Japanese were way ahead of the Koreans in the military sphere. They had some of the newest warships in the world, even if it was only a fraction of what they would build in the decades to come. Japan's power on the seas was no match for Korea. The same held true for Japan's advances in land warfare and weaponry. Korea had no choice but to sign the treaty forced upon it.

As part of the Kanghwa Treaty, Japanese advisers flooded Korea, which both the Koreans and their Chinese neighbors saw as a possible preliminary step toward Japanese colonization of the Korean Peninsula. The Russian Empire also saw Japan as a threat. Not only did Russia have trade interests there, but Korea also bordered Russia. The Korean Peninsula was just a stone's throw across the sea from Russian ports.

One of the criticisms leveled at Japan by Koreans, Chinese, and some Japanese was that the Treaty of Kanghwa and the Japanese treatment of Korea were reminiscent of the West's treatment of Japan in the first decades of contact. To combat that obvious hypocrisy, the Japanese developed the idea that they were spreading a protective net over Korea so that the Europeans and Americans would be kept out. Japan would act as a kind of Asian "big brother," protecting other smaller Asian powers from the West. Of course, the Koreans already had a "big brother" in China, and the Chinese were happy with their trade privileges and the occasional payment of tribute. They did not dictate to the Koreans all that much, and they did not lord their apparent advancement over the Koreans like the Japanese began to do.

For almost two decades, the situation in Korea became increasingly tense. There were acts of anti-Japanese violence and riots. In response, the Japanese made their business terms more difficult and forced the Koreans to pay for damages caused by the riots. In 1894, the Tonghak Rebellion began among the lower classes in Korea. The situation rapidly got out of control, with the Korean government unable to quell the violence. Korea asked China to send troops to help end the rebellion, even though China had meddled in Korean politics for some time. In 1884, a pro-Japanese Korean politician was assassinated in the most brutal way when he visited the Chinese city of Shanghai. Still, the unrest and the Japanese were relative unknowns; the Chinese were not.

Insulted by the anti-Japanese violence, the fact that the Koreans asked the Chinese to help rather than themselves, and the possibility that the Chinese would take over what were now substantial Japanese business interests in Korea, Japan sent a large body of troops. Soon, Chinese and Japanese troops began to fire on each other, starting the First Sino-Japanese War, which lasted from August 1894 to March 1895.

The war lasted for nine months. The world expected China to destroy the Japanese army and navy. Those who allowed themselves to believe that were almost willfully in denial. With some minor exceptions, the Chinese forces facing the Japanese were armed with outmoded bladed weapons, and what few firearms they had were mostly outdated as well. The Chinese navy (which was really a collection of ships belonging to relatively independent and self-interested warlords) outnumbered the Japanese but were almost all wooden or old ironclad steamers with old cannons.

By the spring of 1895, the Japanese had won a number of battles on both sea and land and had marched troops into the mineral-rich Chinese-controlled state of Manchuria. Within nine months, the Chinese military, people, and leadership had been defeated and humiliated. They sued for peace in March 1895.

Due to their victory, the Japanese cemented their position in Korea, and for all intents and purposes, Korea became a Japanese possession. Japan also claimed the island of Taiwan, which they renamed Formosa, and took control of the Liaodong Peninsula in northern coastal mainland China as a territorial concession, something the Europeans had done with other parts of China. China's defeat in the war was one of the direct causes of the overthrow of the imperial system in 1911.

Naturally, the war was popular in Japan. Japan had finally put China in its place after centuries of Chinese dominance in the area. The addition of Taiwan also strengthened Japan's position in the Pacific. Combined with Japan's annexation of the Kingdom of the Ryukyu Islands in 1879, whose main island is Okinawa, Japan had a much greater naval reach in the region than it had just a few years before.

(Also of note is the Japanese government's establishment of a full government bureaucracy on the northern island of Hokkaido, which, for centuries, had been a neglected part of the country and only had settlements on its southern coast. The rest belonged to the indigenous Ainu people, an ethnic group more related to Siberian native tribes than the Japanese. We will talk about the history of

Japan's minorities in a later chapter.)

Illustration 12: Cartoon in British magazine Punch of a small aggressive Japan defeating giant China.

https://en.wikipedia.org/wiki/File:JapanPunch29September1894.jpg

In 1842, the British defeated the Chinese in the First Opium War and would later defeat China in the Second Opium War. This resulted in China agreeing to unfair trade agreements and the ceding of territory to British control (Hong Kong). Other European powers and the United States forced China to agree to the same terms it had given the British, along with what were called concessions—territories governed by the Europeans or their business interests (which were essentially the same thing). These concessions, for the most part, were either large, important sections of Chinese coastal cities or somewhat larger areas that might include more than one city or port. Japan also received concessions in some of China's major cities, most importantly in China's richest city and port, Shanghai.

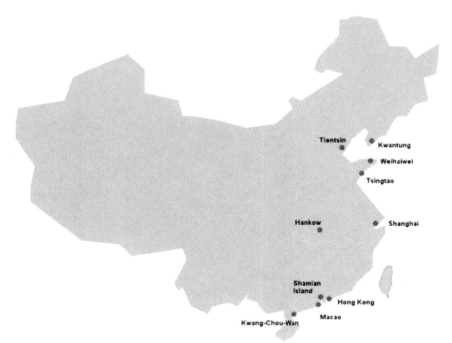

Illustration 13: The main concessions of China in the early 20th century

Russo-Japanese War

Port Arthur was perhaps one of the most important ports; today, it is known as Lushun. Port Arthur was a modern deep-water port that was leased to the Russians by the Chinese and was home to the Pacific Fleet of the Imperial Russian Navy.

When the Japanese defeated China in Korea in 1896, the Russians were quite alarmed, as they had many trade interests in Korea. An aggressive Japan, with concessions in China and control of Korea, was a threat to Russian interests and territories in the Far East. Conversely, the Japanese viewed the strong Russian military presence at Port Arthur, in parts of Manchuria, and on the Korean border as both an economic and military threat to their interests in China, Korea, and their territories of Taiwan and Okinawa. Additionally, the Russians seemed intent on annexing all of resource-rich Manchuria as well.

In 1900, the Boxer Rebellion broke out in China. The English name is derived from the Chinese name for the Society of Righteous Harmonious Fists, the main Chinese paramilitary group that fomented the rebellion, which was aimed at both foreigners in China and the Chinese government for giving up so much territory and sovereignty to foreign powers. The tale of the Boxer Rebellion is long and complicated, but for our purposes here, suffice it to say that the rebels were eventually put down at great cost, and China was forced to cede even more territory. One interesting aspect of the foreign reaction to the rebellion was the somewhat coordinated effort of the Europeans, Americans, and Japanese.

It had been understood that when the Boxer Rebellion was put down, the Russians would remove the additional troops they had brought into Manchuria. However, China was weak, and (according to Russian thinking) no other power was going to risk war with Russia over Manchuria. So, the Russians kept adding troops and lengthening the rail system they had already built, with the obvious aim of controlling all of the vast territories.

Japan, in particular, viewed this situation with alarm and insisted on a fair division of the territories and its riches; weak and divided China was not consulted. Between 1902 and early 1904, a series of talks took place between Russia and Japan. The Russians had the upper hand. They controlled much of the territory, and their strong Pacific Fleet was based nearby. The talks were fruitless, so on February 8th, 1904, the Japanese Imperial Navy attacked the Russian base at Port Arthur, subsequently landing troops and besieging the port. This was a surprise attack—no declaration of war had been made, which international custom called for (at least among the Western powers).

The world was shocked at the brazenness of the Japanese. The Japanese moved down the Liaodong Peninsula toward Port Arthur, coming into cannon range in August. The Japanese fleet, which was under the command of a man who would become a national hero, Togo Heihechiro (better known to history as Admiral Togo—not to be confused with General Tojo, who commanded Japanese forces in WWII), blocked the Russian fleet from moving into the Yellow Sea and the Pacific.

When the Japanese began to shell Port Arthur from land, the Russians attempted to break the Japanese blockade and engage them at sea. This effort was doomed from the start. Admiral Togo had studied naval tactics in England, and his personal hero was the famed British seaman Admiral Horatio Nelson. Actually, Togo believed he was the reincarnation of Nelson, and what he did to the Russians in the Battle of the Yellow Sea on August 10th, 1904, was exactly what Nelson would have done. When the Russians moved toward the Japanese fleet, the Japanese were in a perfect position. They had, in naval parlance, "crossed the T," which allowed all of the guns of their more modern, better-armed, and better-protected fleet to open fire on the Russians while the Russians headed straight for them. The Russians could only bring their forward guns to bear, and they had to be careful not to hit their own ships, which reduced their firepower and caused their gunners to be wildly inaccurate.

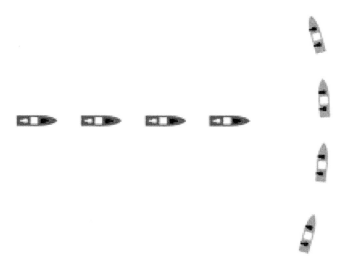

Illustration 14: A simple drawing of the Battle of the Yellow Sea.
Stephan Brunker 2004, This file is licensed under the Creative Commons Attribution-Share Alike 3.0 Unported license; https://en.wikipedia.org/wiki/File:Crossing_the_T.png

The Russians fought bravely but were both outgunned and outmaneuvered. They could not break out into the Yellow Sea, and the ships that were not damaged beyond repair were allowed to be taken under escort to neutral ports nearby, where they and their crews were interned for the rest of the war.

To say the world was shocked by the Japanese victory at Port Arthur is putting it mildly. Still, there were those, including Russian Tsar Nicholas II and his advisers, who believed that the surprise attack had been the deciding factor. When the powerful Russian Baltic Fleet arrived in the Pacific, the outcome would be different, and the Japanese would be "put in their place." That fleet left St. Petersburg when word was received that Port Arthur was besieged with the Pacific Fleet bottled up in the harbor.

While in port in French Madagascar, the Russians learned that the Pacific Fleet had been defeated at Port Arthur. They were determined to make it to their far eastern port of Vladivostok to resupply and evaluate the situation in the Far East before taking action. The Russian Baltic Fleet sailed around the world, facing tremendous logistical problems on the way. They finally arrived in the Sea of Japan in late May 1905 and decided that the best way to Vladivostok was the shortest and most direct route. Unfortunately, this was also the most dangerous route, as it would force the Russian fleet to sail between Japan and Korea through the Tsushima Strait.

Illustration 15: Admiral Togo in later life.
https://en.wikipedia.org/wiki/File:T%C5%8Dg%C5%8D_Heihachir%C5%8D.jpg

The Russians elected to make their voyage through the strait at night, but unfortunately, adherence to the international rules of war meant the two hospital ships sailing with the fleet had to remain illuminated. An armed Japanese merchant vessel observed this and sent a wireless message (technology the Russians did not have yet) to the main Japanese fleet. It immediately made its way toward the enemy and was informed throughout the night about the enemy's location. Once again, Admiral Togo was able to "cross the T," and this time, the result was absolutely devastating. The Russians lost virtually their entire fleet, including the eight battleships that were their pride. Five thousand Russian sailors lost their lives. Three smaller vessels made it to Vladivostok, and six more were interned at neutral ports under Japanese escort. The Japanese lost three small torpedo boats and just under 120 dead. Once again, the Japanese had shocked the world, and that's putting it very mildly.

The end of the war was brokered by another rising world power, the United States of America, which resulted in President Theodore Roosevelt winning the Nobel Peace Prize for his efforts. The Treaty of Portsmouth gave Japan the Liaodong Peninsula and Port Arthur (again, the Chinese were not asked for their opinion), the southern half of Sakhalin Island (which lies just north of Hokkaido and is today completely owned by Russia), and control of the main railroad in Manchuria, though Manchuria itself was returned to China. Korea was recognized as a Japanese possession.

For Russia, the war was a humiliating disaster and directly led to the weakening of the tsarist system and its eventual overthrow in 1917. The Japanese had arrived on the world scene, and Admiral Togo was hailed as the "Japanese Nelson," but something about the victory left many Japanese feeling empty. Part of that feeling had to do with Japan not receiving what traditionally occurred after a conflict: a large cash indemnity. Many Japanese believed they should have been awarded all of Sakhalin Island as well, and as a result, there were riots in the streets of a number of Japanese cities. In the Diet (Japan's legislative body), there were rumblings against the continued high levels of military spending, which came at the expense of social programs, important improvements in transportation within the cities, and the production of rice.

These protests were a reflection of a growing movement in the country, something that other industrial powers were dealing with as well. It was the growth of socialism in its many forms. In 1901, the Social Democratic Party was founded in Japan. It was based on the ideas of the same types of parties in Europe, especially the influential Social Democrats in Germany. Generally speaking, the Social Democrats in both countries were pushing for greater rights for workers, the right to organize unions, and less spending on the military and more spending on domestic issues, which included health insurance, industrial safety, and a bigger social safety net (unemployment insurance, etc.).

The Social Democratic Party in Germany was sidelined by the German Kaiser and his powerful chancellor, Otto von Bismarck, though it was the largest party in the country. The ruling elite in Japan, which was made up of military men (mostly from old samurai families) and the increasingly powerful industrial elite, took the German model one step further—they outlawed the party. This forced many of those within the Social Democrats to take a harder line, and many converted to either communism or anarchism, both of which were illegal and underground.

Over the course of the first two decades of the 20th century, Japan (Tokyo in particular) was the site of frequent protests against government policies and the extremely powerful corporations, the largest of which had formed what is known in Japanese history as the *zaibatsu*. The United States was going through the end stages of its own struggles with its *zaibatsu*, otherwise known as trusts or monopolies.

In Japan, many of the large corporations (Mitsubishi, Mitsui, and Sumitomo, for example) worked in close coordination with the government. In quite a few instances, they were powerful enough economically to force government action, including actions against the nascent labor movement. Though military spending declined for most of the 1920s in favor of domestic projects, the military and the *zaibatsu* worked together in secret against both the influence of the Diet and the imperial court. In the late 1920s, the military inched closer and closer to having complete control of the government. The *zaibatsu* acted as almost another branch of the military and sought military help in keeping their workers in line as

Japan headed toward WWII.

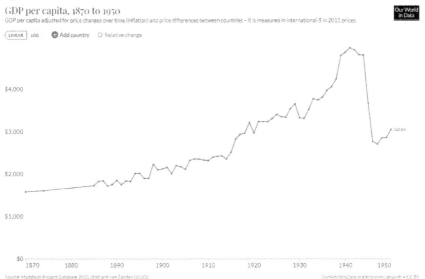

GDP per capita, 1870 to 1950

GDP per capita adjusted for price changes over time (inflation) and price differences between countries - it is measured in international-$ in 2011 prices.

Source: Maddison Project Database 2020 (Bolt and van Zanden (2020))   OurWorldInData.org/economic-growth • CC BY

Illustration 16: Japanese per capita GDP, 1870–1950. Between 1870 and the outbreak of World War II with the US in 1941, Japan's economy almost quadrupled.

Max Roser, This file is licensed under the Creative Commons Attribution-Share Alike 4.0 International license;<https://creativecommons.org/licenses/by-sa/4.0/deed.en> https://en.wikipedia.org/wiki/File:GDP_per_capita_of_Japan_1870_to_1950.jpg

Under Meiji and his successors, Japan went from an economically backward, isolated nation to a world power in the space of forty years. To many, the Meiji era is Japan's "golden age," and it is easy to understand why.

Chapter 4 – The Taisho Era

Emperor Meiji died on July 29th, 1912, after a long, successful, but painfully unhealthy life. His funeral was a national day of mourning, and the emperor was honored with many titles posthumously—one of them being the imperial era name "Meiji" for "enlightened rule." Still, when he died, many liberal-minded Japanese were relieved. Like many rulers as they age, Meiji had grown increasingly conservative, almost attempting to keep in place the many evolutionary changes he had helped bring about beginning in 1868. As you have read, history waits for no one, and the Japanese had firsthand knowledge of what happened when a country stagnated.

Illustration 17: The funeral procession of Emperor Meiji, 1912.
https://en.wikipedia.org/wiki/File:Funeral_of_Emperor_Meiji_5.JPG

Emperor Meiji's son, Yoshihito (who became Emperor Taisho upon his death in 1926, with "Taisho" meaning "great righteousness"), reigned from 1912 to 1926. "Reigned" is used loosely here, as Emperor Taisho had a number of strikes against him. Some say he was mentally challenged, but those might have been assumptions stemming from his appearance and physical infirmities, which manifested themselves in twitching and a peculiar gait. He was kept from sight as much as possible by the members of the imperial household and often gave his speeches from behind a screen (as had been tradition before the Meiji era) so people would not see his "weaknesses." The emperor was married to a woman from the Fujiwara clan, one of the oldest and most prestigious clans. She was chosen for her grace, intelligence, and happy disposition— all things that Yoshihito seemingly lacked.

Taisho is a relatively forgotten personality today. He was not inclined to rule and preferred to spend his time learning languages (he did appear to have a proclivity for them) rather than attend meetings or learn about policy. When the emperor's input or presence was needed, Taisho was instructed on what position to take by the remaining *genro* (those five leading samurai who had surrounded and guided Meiji), the generals and admirals, or his powerful chamberlain. In many cases, these three groups worked together, making it even more difficult for the emperor to have his own voice, which he was not truly interested in having anyway.

The Taisho era is remembered much more for the changes in Japanese society than for its namesake.

One of the more interesting aspects of the Taisho era was the rise of democratic ideas in Japan. Though the Meiji era saw the formation of the Japanese parliament, the Diet, it was more of an advisory body to the emperor and those around him. It also gave the more powerful segments of Japanese society a finger on the pulse, for the members of the Diet were elected officials but were elected by landowning males only.

The Meiji era saw, especially at its end, a growth of control in the military and the *zaibatsu*. However, by 1912, when Meiji died, the Japanese people, especially those in the large cities, were no longer the isolated and insular people they had been before the arrival of Matthew Perry. Even if they were not in direct contact with the outside world through business (and most were not), the Japanese were increasingly aware of happenings around the world through the many newspapers in the country and the growth of the radio industry in the first part of the 20th century. This meant that, at least in the cities, the citizens of Japan were aware of life in Western democracies, especially in the United States. Throughout the later 1910s and most of the 1920s, many Japanese looked at America as a role model, politically, economically, and culturally.

The new emperor's era is also known as the period of Taisho Democracy. The position of the emperor gradually reverted to the status of a figurehead, and the emperor did not take part in the reforms that were attempted and/or enacted during his reign. However, increasing numbers of liberal-minded intellectuals, from writers to university professors, came to lead or influence Japanese political and cultural thought. Two of them were Yoshino Sakuzo and Nitobe Inazo.

Yoshino was an influential history professor and student of political science. His reputation for brilliance was so well known that after graduation, he was hired by the most powerful warlord in China, Yuan Shikai, as a personal tutor for three years. When Yoshino returned to Japan, he began teaching at his alma mater and wrote his most influential book, *On the Meaning of Constitutional Government*, in 1916. In his book, he argued that democracy need not eliminate or sideline the emperor and that Japan could build a representative democracy somewhere along the lines of Great Britain or Germany (though the German equivalent of parliamentary democracy was nowhere near as democratic as the United Kingdom at the time).

During the late 1910s and early 1920s, the Japanese worked on integrating Japan into the world order that emerged after World War I. Nitobe Inazo was one of the most notable Japanese who worked on this. He was a pacifist Quaker who was introduced to the sect by his future wife, the American Mary Elkington. A pacifist and Quaker who married a foreigner was a rarity in Japan at the time, to say the least.

Inazo was an early advocate for participation in the new League of Nations, the precursor to today's United Nations, and became an undersecretary general of the League from 1920 to 1930 before a resurgent military forced Japan to quit the League. He was also a founding member of the forerunner of today's UNESCO, which attempts to ensure education is available to every child and citizen of the world.

Much of this movement toward some sort of democracy was powered by the changes in the Japanese workplace. Like many of the factories in Europe and North America, issues like worker representation, safety, medical insurance, and unionization were at the forefront. Some changes were made, though not nearly enough to satisfy many of the workers on the factory floor.

Another change that eventually impacted the Japanese economy and life was the rise of the famous Japanese salaryman. Beginning in the 1960s and 1970s and continuing today, the salaryman is one of the first images that come to mind when thinking about Japan. In Taisho's Japan, the rise of the white-collar salaryman was just beginning. As time went by, the salarymen would both push for changes in the corporate structures of Japan and work to secure them.

Though there were large numbers of poorer and poorly educated women who worked in many of the factories of Japan, more and more middle-class women were working in white-collar jobs, though the overwhelming majority worked in menial or subordinate positions.

One of the white-collar jobs dominated by women was shopkeeping, especially in the larger, more cosmopolitan cities. Quite a few of these shops and stands sold books or magazines. While the work was tedious and did not pay much, the women who worked at them were exposed not only to the information they were selling but also to the many conversations about current events that took place around them.

Many of these women called themselves *modan garu* (the Japanese pronunciation of "modern girls") or *moga* for short. The *moga* were a largely urban phenomena and highly influenced by images and stories from abroad. The height of the *moga* movement and fashion was in the mid-1920s when the US flapper culture took root in Japan, as did jazz music, baseball, and a general feeling that women should have more rights.

Like other developed nations of the time, Japan saw an intense growth in artistic output. A great deal of the illustrative arts was decidedly "un-Japanese," meaning Western in style, or a part of the popular abstract modern art movement of the time (think Picasso). But probably the greatest expression of "new" Japan was in the literary field. Tanizaki Junichiro and Akutagawa Ryunosuke, perhaps the most famous and exalted authors in the history of 20th-century Japan, wrote about great social changes in their country. Most of their works reflected some of the deeper questions many Japanese were asking themselves, such as "What does it mean to be Japanese in this new world?" and "What is the relationship of the individual to the state or corporation?" The Japanese reflected on some of the trends going on in Europe and the US and experimented with new forms of poetry that were decidedly non-traditional compared to the Japanese poetry of the past one thousand years.

Though manga's real popularity was not to come until the 1950s with the works of Osamu Tezuka, a new and unique form of Japanese artistic expression began its rise during the 1920s. Manga is graphic fiction that one can see almost everywhere now, from magazines to movies to TV. It began as a way to engage salarymen on their way to work and explain some of the social and political issues of the day to both those with little leisure time and those less-educated.

The First World War

Before we get too far into the 1920s, let's stop and take a look at Japan's role in World War One. Military and other historians, especially in the United States, often point out that Japan was one of the Allied powers during the war, along with Great Britain, France, Russia (its recent enemy), Italy, and the United States. This is true, but Japan did not fight the war for the same reasons as the others. Now, of course, most wars have many factors involved; they don't typically involve only territorial aggrandizement and political power. Economics and other questions, such as global prestige and influence, come into play. In Europe, the war began over the control and influence of the Balkan Peninsula (Serbia, Bosnia, etc.), but it was also a war between liberal democracies in France and

Great Britain versus absolute monarchy. Though Russia was both an absolute monarchy and an Allied power, its distance and lack of influence in Europe were essentially overlooked. Thus, the war was a Western conflict, and Japan played a secondary role at best.

However, for the Japanese, the war, in terms of territorial gains and influence, was a boon. The decision to enter the war on the side of the Allies was a pragmatic one. Most of the colonies in Asia were in the hands of either the French or British (with the exception of the Dutch East Indies, today's Indonesia, but Holland was a neutral nation in WWI). Russian holdings were minimal, especially after the Russo-Japanese War, and so were Germany's. What's more, the Germans had very little manpower in their Pacific and Chinese territories and few ships to protect and supply them. The French and British did. The Japanese handled the Russians relatively easily in the Russo-Japanese War, but they were not going to rival French and British military power (especially at sea) for some time.

Thus, the decision was made to join the Allies. The addition of the Japanese fleet to help protect Allied colonies from German raiders would allow the British and French to shift both navies and manpower to Europe, where they were more desperately needed. This also meant the Japanese were able to seize, with very little trouble, many of the German colonies in the Pacific, such as the Marshall Islands, Caroline Island, and the Mariana Islands in the north-central Pacific and half of the large island of New Guinea, which is north of Australia. A three-month-long siege of the German concession city of Tsingtao resulted in a Japanese victory and its control of another chunk of Chinese territory.

In 1917, the Japanese sent a number of vessels to help escort British merchantmen in the Mediterranean (though truth be told, the real threat of the Imperial German Navy had passed by 1917, at least in the Mediterranean), and they sent a number of troops to the Murmansk Peninsula of Russia along with Britain, France, and the US in a strange and abortive attempt to help the anti-communist Whites during the Russian Revolution.

When calm was restored after the war, some of the more forward-thinking military officers and strategists among the British and Americans realized that it was possible that a new and aggressive Japan might have just expanded into vast areas of the Pacific, potentially posing a threat to both Western powers. They were right, as you will read in our section on World War II.

Japan sent a full delegation to the Paris Peace Conference, which officially ended WWI. However, they weren't consulted nearly as much as they had wanted to be. Many Japanese believed it was because of racial bias (and it partly was, for the Western Powers decidedly rebuffed Japan's suggestion of a racial equality clause in the Preamble to the Covenant of the League of Nations). But Italy was also an ally and had supplied hundreds of thousands of men to the Allied cause at great cost in lives and treasure. Except for some very public photo opportunities, the Italians were essentially dismissed in the same way as the Japanese. The Americans, British, and French ran the show.

Still, Japan had "arrived" on the international scene and had gained some strategically placed islands in the Pacific. These islands were not of any great value as far as resources went, but they could be incredibly important naval supply and staging bases, either to defend Japan far from the home islands or to make it easier to attack potential enemies (Holland with the oil-rich East Indies, the UK and its commonwealth, and the growing power of the United States, which had control of the Philippines and a number of Pacific islands).

The omission of the racial equality clause caused great anger in Japan. Riots took place. Westerners were assaulted in a few instances. Combined with the dueling Japanese reactions to the Washington Naval Conference, which followed on the heels of the Treaty of Versailles and the formation of the League of Nations, public opinion in much of Japan, especially within the military and the political right-wing, grew increasingly anti-Western. However, it would take a good ten years of internal tumult and violence for anti-Westernism to become government policy.

In the first two decades of the 20th century, Japan had a population surplus, and immigration (especially of those in the lower classes) was seen as a way of relieving its overpopulation, especially in the cities. The implementation of laws in the United States that prohibited the immigration of people from Asia (specifically Japan and China) added fuel to the anti-Western and anti-American feelings that would grow to dangerous proportions in the early 1940s.

In 1922, Japan and the leading Western powers (minus the new Soviet Union) signed the Washington Naval Treaty, which had been convened to lessen the potential for another arms race that could lead to war. Many nations during the 1920s wanted to cut back on defense spending after WWI and invest both money and manpower in economic recovery and growth after the conflict.

Japan's participation is interesting. As a great power, Japan naturally wanted to be part of any worldwide agreements or at least be privy to the talks that led to them. Domestically, many Japanese wanted their government to spend less on arms and more on infrastructure. However, many of those same Japanese (and quite a few more) wanted to make sure that Japan's military, especially its navy, was at least as strong as the other powers in the Pacific. They got what they wanted, but many misinterpreted the final result as an insult to Japanese honor. (Remember, the days of the samurai and their willingness to die or kill themselves for honor were still fresh in the memory of many Japanese, especially the senior leadership of the military.)

Beginning history students learn that the Washington Naval Conference, at least as far as it concerned Japan, ended with the formula "5-5-3." This referenced the tonnage of battleships permitted to Great Britain, the United States, and Japan: 525,000 tons for Britain and the US and 300,000 tons for Japan. Given that both the US and Great Britain had interests all over the world while Japan's sphere of naval influence was in the Pacific, in many ways, this was a good deal for the Japanese. Some saw it that way, as the Japanese would have parity in the Pacific (by the way, France and Italy, which both had interests in the Atlantic and Pacific, were accorded less tonnage than the Japanese were). Still, the numbers rankled the Japanese, not necessarily because of what they meant but because of how they looked: "5-5" for the West and "3" for the Japanese. Many in the growing number of far right-cliques in Japan used this as a recruiting tool within the armed forces, along with the Westerners' dismissal of the equality clause in the Covenant of the League of Nations.

In 1926, Yoshihito died and became Emperor Taisho. His son, Hirohito, took the imperial Chrysanthemum Throne. The flower has been the symbol of the imperial family since before 1000 CE.

Chapter 5 – The Early Showa Era, 1926–1945

Isaac Newton's third law of motion states that "for every action, there is an equal and opposite reaction." This holds just as true for current events and history as it does for movement. Actually, in many ways, it's simpler to think of human development and history as movement itself—sometimes it moves quickly, sometimes it moves slowly. There are eddies in which no movement is perceived (for instance, the economic situation of the Great Depression) but which, under the surface, moves nonetheless.

Beginning history majors spend a great deal of time studying the French Revolution. In those twenty-odd years, change and the reaction to it happened so quickly and sometimes so exactly and radically that it is relatively easy to understand how Newton's law applies to more than the physical reaction that happens when a ball is thrown or a cannon is fired.

This process of change and reaction was especially pronounced in Japan during the 1910s and 1920s. As you read in the last chapter, this period saw Japan finally arrive on the international world stage, and many changes took place within Japanese society, especially among the urban lower and middle classes.

Illustration 18: Hirohito in 1935.
https://commons.wikimedia.org/wiki/File:Emperor_Showa_in_dress.jpg

Small but incremental changes in the workplace, changes in the education system, the position of women, moving away from exorbitant military spending, and an interest in the culture of the United States were some of the many changes taking place in Japan when Hirohito took the throne in 1926. Hirohito, much like his father, was quiet and bookish, though with none of the infirmities. His interest was botany. By the end of his long life and reign in 1989, the emperor had been recognized as one of the leading botanists in the world and had published many articles on the subject in leading academic journals.

We will refer to him solely as Hirohito for the rest of this book. However, this emperor is known as Emperor Showa in Japan. "Showa" ironically means "enlightened peace," which is based more on the emperor's later years when he supported the American-imposed demilitarization of Japan rather than his reign's tremendously warlike period.

Debate continues as to how much of a role Hirohito played in Japan's drive for domination in Asia and the Pacific in the 1930s and 1940s. At the very least, he was complicitly silent during the majority of those years, though his one memorable direct and very public order ended WWII in the Pacific (and, of course, the threat of Japan's nuclear annihilation, which might have been the only reason he did it). What we know for sure is that in the 1930s and 1940s, he did nothing to slow Japan's attempt to dominate about half the world.

While many of the changes mentioned in the previous chapter grabbed headlines, not only in Japan but also in the West, there was a slowly boiling and eventually seething resentment of the direction that Japan seemed to take. Western clothes, music, sports, and liberal attitude toward women (though hardly progressive by today's standards) were seen by many Japanese as straying further from the Japanese identity that had been formed over the course of more than one thousand years.

These feelings were especially acute in military circles, more so in the army than the navy, though the navy had its share of reactionaries. The military was especially sensitive to what it deemed as "insults to Japanese honor," such as the dismissive attitude of the Western powers at Versailles after WWI, the rejection of the racial equality clause in the League of Nations Preamble, the Washington Naval Conference, and the passage of anti-Asian immigration laws in the US. (To be fair, these were seen in Japan through a rather narrow lens; most Japanese conservatives would have been satisfied with the Americans allowing Japanese immigration but limiting that of other Asian nations.)

To a degree, the changes happening in Japan during the 1920s and early 1930s mirrored those taking place in Germany, with their most significant shared traits being a growing anti-democratic and nationalistic undercurrent, which eventually grew to dominate both nations.

In 1929, the onset of the Great Depression exacerbated these anti-foreign feelings. When the New York Stock Exchange crashed, it set off a chain reaction around the globe. Though there were many causes of the Great Depression, the "Crash of '29" was the straw that broke the proverbial camel's back. In Japan, the economic situation had been made worse by the devastating earthquake of 1923, which claimed an estimated 100,000-plus deaths and caused extensive damage in Tokyo. In 1931, Japan's currency crashed by 50 percent against the dollar, and unemployment in Japan reached 20 percent or more within months after the Wall Street Crash.

Economic troubles, especially severe ones, always lead to political strife. While the rest of the world had many of the same issues as Japan, the Japanese struggled with an additional one: Should Japan have been in such a rush to "Westernize" and become part of a global power structure that was dominated by the Europeans and Americans? Throughout the 1930s, more and more Japanese began to answer "no."

The intellectual class of Japan, many of whom once sang the praises of Westernization and modernity, now began to decry Japan's embrace of Western culture. Though most Japanese recognized that its rapid industrialization had allowed it to become a world power, many began to question capitalism itself, at least as it existed at that time. This did not mean that the elites of Japan turned to communism as a solution (though communism, which was outlawed in 1925, did gain popularity in the workplace and universities as an underground movement). Instead, many began to look for another way, which eventually turned into a Japanese form of fascism. The military and corporations worked hand in hand, both in terms of production and national aims. The military also helped to keep a very tight lid on workers' rights and movements.

Though there was an underground movement on the political left advocating for socialism, the left was never a real danger in Japan. The real danger was on the right, where various cliques of military officers in the Imperial Japanese Army and Imperial Japanese Navy worked to overthrow what they believed was a succession of Western-style governments in the last part of the 1920s and especially in the early 1930s. Sometimes, these cliques worked separately, unknown to each other, and sometimes, their efforts were coordinated.

The 1930s are known as the period of "government by assassination." In 1930, Prime Minister Hamaguchi Osachi, a liberal-leaning politician, was shot by an ultra-nationalist group and eventually succumbed to his wounds. The excuse given by his killers was that Osachi had failed to rectify the "unfair" Washington Naval Treaty with the Western powers. Sadly and ironically, Osachi was shot in the exact same spot that Prime Minister Hara Takashi (the first commoner, meaning one with no samurai roots, and the first Christian prime minister in Japanese history) had been killed nine years earlier by a right-wing railroad worker.

In 1931, police and more moderate elements of the intelligence service uncovered plans for two separate coups d'état among right-wing extremists. In 1932, Osachi's successor, Inukai Tsuyoshi, was killed by a group of naval officers for the lack of support he showed for the Japanese army's invasion of Manchuria, which had been a totally unsanctioned operation.

In Tokyo and other major cities, a large segment of the population was repulsed and angered by these events and other acts of violence by right-wing cliques within the military. However, there was growing support for them in the conservative countryside, which had been bypassed and forgotten by the changes taking place in the more liberal cities. Even among people who believed the military had grown too influential, there was a feeling of pride due to Japan's success and colonization of Manchuria. However, many previously moderate Japanese turned to the right when the world, as represented by the League of Nations, condemned Japan's invasion of Manchuria. The Japanese representatives of that body dramatically stood up and left, never to return. After the March 1932 assassination of Prime Minister Inukai Tsuyoshi, the military had begun to run the country, and its influence and rule grew throughout the decade. No prime minister was able to rule Japan without following the dictates of the military. So, the emperor remained silent.

Manchuria/Manchukuo

Today, Manchuria is the northernmost province of China. In 1931, it was an autonomous region of China, ostensibly with its own government, but in reality, it was dominated by Chinese warlords who were at best corrupt and at worst corrupt and incompetent. It's important to know that China itself was splintered politically and regionally. In the eastern regions along the coast and especially in the cities, the Nationalist Party of China (or Kuomintang, which still exists in Taiwan) attempted to govern a huge population and area. The leader of the Kuomintang was Generalissimo Chiang Kai-shek, who had been a protégé of the first Republican leader of China, Dr. Sun Yat-sen.

Unfortunately for Chiang, his hold on power outside the coastal areas was tenuous at best. He had to contend with three other groups in his attempt to centralize the country under his control: the Western powers (including Japan), the warlords (military officers who had carved out their own areas of control in various parts of the nation, some of them vast and powerful), and the communists (who were increasingly under the control of Mao Zedong, who would lead the communists to victory in the civil war that followed WWII).

The Japanese took advantage of these divisions in their conquest of Manchuria, which they renamed "Manchukuo" after their takeover, and later in their invasion of China itself. One interesting thing about the Japanese invasion of Manchuria was that it was not sanctioned by the government or the bulk of the military hierarchy in Tokyo.

The attack on Manchuria was the brainchild of a charismatic and peculiar Japanese colonel named Ishiwara Kanji. Ishiwara was the field commander of the Japanese Kwantung Army (named for the Manchurian Kwantung Peninsula, where its headquarters were located and the site of the aforementioned Port Arthur, which had been won by the Japanese in the Russo-Japanese War). Among the military hierarchy in Tokyo, Ishiwara was considered a brilliant but dangerous and unstable officer. He claimed to have visions of the "end of the world," or at least of the end of the world as it existed at that time. This vision called for Ishiwara to lead Japan into a war from which it would (of course) emerge victorious and usher in a new age of humanity based on what he called "non-selfish" principles. These principles were more along the lines of the Japanese samurai code of service and Buddhist ideals rather than communism, which virtually everyone in the Japanese military hated.

At the end of the Russo-Japanese War, Japan was awarded control of the Southern Manchurian Railway, which was important to allow resources and trade goods to come in and out of the Japanese-controlled Kwantung Peninsula. A small group of Ishiwara's men planted explosives along a section of track near a local Manchurian army base. They intended to blame the Chinese for the action, hoping that the Imperial General Staff in Tokyo would use this as a reason to launch an invasion of Manchuria. The explosion and the damage it caused were laughably small and insignificant, but local Japanese journalists (along with a number of Western reporters) were hustled to the site to take pictures of the damage, which Ishiwara insisted was the work of the Chinese. To prove this, a number of pieces of "evidence" with Chinese script had been strewn about the area. None of the Western journalists believed the explosion was carried out by the Chinese, and even some of the Japanese reporters had their doubts, but they dutifully reported what Ishiwara suggested they report. By the time their sensational reports reached Tokyo, Ishiwara's Kwantung Army had launched an attack on the nearby Chinese base and had taken over most of the territory within a short amount of time.

In Japan, debate raged within the military. As you read above, Prime Minister Inukai was assassinated for his lack of support for the operation, and within the Imperial General Staff, there were those who feared that Ishiwara's actions would lead to a wider war, one that Japan might not be able to win. There was also the condemnation of Ishiwara himself for taking matters into his own hands and acting without instruction. Some also believed that it was high time for Japan to expand into mineral-rich Asia and restore some of the martial spirit of the samurai to Japanese life.

Within a short time, all of Manchuria was under Japanese control. The last Chinese emperor, Pu Yi (made famous in the West by the 1987 film *The Last Emperor*), was made the head of the puppet state of Manchukuo under a Japanese military government. Ishiwara believed that many Japanese would applaud his "conquest," and to a large degree, that was true, especially in the darkened mood of the Great Depression. But Prime Minister Inukai Tsuyoshi was assassinated for his condemnation of the Manchurian incident. Hirohito voiced no objections, but he, like his father before him, was effectively sidelined politically.

In 1933, the League of Nations released the Lytton Report, which investigated Japan's actions in Manchuria. The report condemned the invasion as being fully the responsibility of the Japanese. The invasion was also deemed an "aggressive war," which was banned by the League of Nations Charter. The report and the League demanded the Japanese withdraw their troops from Manchuria. Japan responded to that demand by simply walking out of the League in February, never to return. Many view Japan's rejection of the League as its death knell. Later that year, the new German chancellor, Adolf Hitler, withdrew Germany from the League as he had long promised to do. Hitler had seen that there had been no real international consequences for Japan, though the League Charter called on the world to impose them.

To Japan and its people, the League of Nations was hypocritical. Many accused it of being racially biased, which was not an unfounded charge, and many Japanese pointed out that the European powers had seized much of the world by force (some, especially in the Middle East, rather recently). But when it came to Japan and Asia, things were different; the League acted as a regional organization designed to keep Japan and Asia as a whole reined it.

Two of the consequences of Japan's withdrawal from the League did not necessarily come from any direct action the organization took against it but as a general result of Japan's growing isolation. First, Japan had to increase its military spending to defend itself against any Western or Chinese moves. Second, this increase in military spending and building was going to necessitate immense resources, most of which Japan did not have in sufficient quantities, especially iron, steel, and coal. Japan had enough of these minerals to begin the first stages of its industrialization in the 19th century, but as Japanese industry and infrastructure grew, more and more resources were needed. Japan had to look elsewhere for them. This was one justification used by the military and its supporters for invading resource-rich Manchuria. As far as petroleum and gasoline, Japan had virtually none of its own and was reliant on imports from the Dutch East Indies and, more importantly (both quantitatively and politically), the United States. Fortunately for Japan, the worldwide economic decline caused by the Great Depression meant that both Holland and the US, despite their own trepidation, continued selling oil, steel, and coal to the Japanese, although this changed in 1940.

By 1938, Japan's military was receiving 75 percent of the national budget. This naturally came at a cost to domestic spending, which caused discontent in many circles. This discontent, however, was kept quiet by custom, history, and force. History dies hard, and the Tokugawa shogunate had almost perfected the totalitarian state before the concept was even developed in writing. The even longer history of Japanese class consciousness and desire for national harmony and unity kept many Japanese quiet. They either wrestled with their conscience or slowly bowed down to the constant militaristic nationalism of the 1930s.

Japan took the final step toward a complete military dictatorship in the second half of the 1930s. In 1936, a small faction within the Japanese military in Tokyo staged a coup. They assassinated the finance minister and a former prime minister and attempted to assassinate the current prime minister but killed his brother in a case of mistaken identity. They also seized control of central Tokyo and issued a demand that the emperor be returned to his rightful place at the top of Japan's political order. Unfortunately, this group, known as the Kodoha or "Imperial Way Faction," shocked and angered the emperor, who saw the coup as both a violation of the Meiji Constitution and a disruption of national harmony.

Within a few days, the coup in Tokyo was quashed by the larger and far more powerful Toseiha or "Control Faction" of the military, which then strengthened its own position in the government. One of the members of the Control Faction was the future prime minister, Hideki Tojo (1884–1948), who became minister of the army in 1938 and was an advocate of Japanese imperial expansion. By the summer of 1937, the military was in charge of Japan, despite having a distant relation of the emperor placed as prime minister (Prince

Konoe Fumimaro, himself an advocate of expansion).

Illustration 19: Tojo (light uniform at center) with his cabinet after being made prime minister in 1941.
https://en.wikipedia.org/wiki/File:Hideki_T%C5%8Dj%C5%8D_Cabinet_19411018.jpg

The Real Beginning of World War II

In July 1937, the Japanese military along the Manchurian-Chinese border provoked another "incident." The Marco Polo Bridge Incident set off a conflict in China that claimed upward of ten to twenty *million* lives and led to the assaults on British, French, Dutch, and American possessions in the Pacific in 1940 and 1941.

The Marco Polo Bridge Incident and its ostensible start by the Chinese led to a massive Japanese push down the eastern coast of China, the most populous nation on Earth then as it is now. Why did the Japanese believe they could successfully invade a nation so much larger than them in both population and size? As you read earlier, China in the late 1920s and 1930s was poor, corrupt, and divided. The Japanese believed they could exploit these weaknesses to their benefit, which they did.

One aspect of Japan's war in both Asia and the Pacific that is often overlooked is the racial and ethnic superiority of the Japanese. In Korea, which Japan had controlled for twenty years before its invasion of China, many Japanese called the Koreans "garlic-eaters," a pejorative term aimed at their dietary habits. In return, the taller

Koreans dubbed the Japanese "dwarves." There was no love lost between the two, and the same feelings carried over to China. The Japanese looked down on the Chinese for being weak and allowing the Europeans to dominate them, as well as their corruption and overpopulated and dirty cities.

The Japanese carried out a genocidal policy, though it was not an organized extermination campaign like what took place under the Nazis in Europe. However, the name of the official Japanese policy in China was named *Jinmetsu Sakusen*, or "The Burn to Ash" strategy. This policy was more commonly referred to by the Japanese as the "Three Alls Policy" for "Kill All, Burn All, Loot All." And that's exactly what they did.

Initially, the Japanese did not intend to conquer all of China. They sought to control the coast. Most of the people lived there, which meant most of China's industries and cities were located there. Things went well for the Japanese in the beginning. The Chinese army under Chiang Kai-shek, for the most part, was poorly trained and equipped compared to the invaders. On top of this, there had been an escalation in the bloody fighting between Chiang Kai-shek's Nationalists and Mao Zedong's Communists since 1934, which resulted in the Communists' famous "Long March." The Japanese were aided by Chiang's seeming determination to fight the Communists rather than mount a stiff opposition to the Japanese.

That began to change with the Battle of Shanghai in the late summer/early fall of 1937. Sometimes called the "Stalingrad of the East" by historians, the battle for China's most populous city was a bloody street battle that ended in a costly Japanese victory. The unexpected resistance in Shanghai, combined with the ethnic and militaristic sense of superiority of the Japanese, was a direct cause of the next battle: the Battle of Nanking (now known as Nanjing).

Nanking was the capital of China. In peacetime, the population was somewhere in the neighborhood of more than half a million, and that was before refugees started to stream in to escape the approaching Japanese. The Japanese advanced on the city on December 9th, 1937, and demanded the Chinese surrender, which they refused. By December 12th, the city was in Japanese hands. Then, the horror began.

The episode is known to history as the "Rape of Nanking." It's estimated that at least twenty thousand Chinese women (including the elderly and girls) were forcibly violated. Many of them were killed afterward and sickeningly, sometimes during. If that were not horrible enough, Japanese soldiers went on a spree of bloody atrocities, encouraged by their officers who also participated in the crimes. These included beheading contests, pyramids of skulls, mass burning of Chinese civilians while they were still alive, and much else that simply staggers the imagination.

Estimates of the number of victims vary from low post-war Japanese estimates (which can be dismissed out of hand) to high estimates from the Chinese, both in Beijing and Taiwan. The number of dead is estimated to be somewhere between 200,000 and 400,000 people; this discrepancy has mostly to do with poor record-keeping of the population before the battle, the transient and destructive nature of war, and the flight of refugees into the city. Needless to say, no matter which number is cited, the Rape of Nanking was one of the most vicious atrocities of the war, not only in Asia but also worldwide. And the sad thing? This type of behavior was not unusual for the Japanese in China. Their campaign ultimately included the use of poison gas, biological weapons, and a truly horrific experimentation center known as "Unit 731," which subjected prisoners (mostly Chinese but also Americans and other Westerners as the war spread) to experiments so horrific they are best left to your imagination.

(You can read much more about the Sino-Japanese War in Captivating History's *The Second Sino-Japanese War* and *The Rape of Nanking*, both of which are available on Amazon.)

Over time, foreign aid to the Chinese increased. (Oddly enough, one of their main suppliers of military weapons and equipment was Germany, which continued, for a time, under Hitler. Many pictures of Chinese troops at the time show them in German-style "coal-scuttle" helmets.) Aid mostly came from the United States, although Britain also helped. However, from 1937 to 1940, Western aid to China did not make any appreciable difference, as it came in very limited quantities. Japan also famously attacked an American river patrol boat in China, the *Panay*, which the Japanese declared was an accident. The Japanese government paid an indemnity to the US and the families of those who were killed, but after the war, it was discovered that the attack on the American vessel was a deliberate message to the US: "keep out, or else."

The West condemned the Japanese invasion and announced the atrocities committed by their military, but the Western powers did virtually nothing to help the Chinese until they were dragged into the war by Japan's actions. The Great Depression and the memory of the losses of WWI still lingered in the West, and many British, French, and American politicians and citizens did not want to be part of a war halfway around the world. The United States had never entered the League of Nations and was not bound by its instructions to defend other nations against aggression, but France and Britain were. Their lack of action gave Adolf Hitler the impetus to begin his war.

World War Two in the Pacific

There was a built-in problem with the Japanese military's plan for the expansion of their empire. Japan was resource-poor and an island nation. The resources Japan lacked were the ones it needed the most. Without iron, coal, steel, and oil, the movements of the Japanese military, especially its navy, would grind to a halt.

Unfortunately, there was a bit of a catch-22 involved. To acquire the resources needed to maintain a modern army and navy, the Japanese needed to conquer or control resources far from home. To ensure the steady flow of these resources, Japan had to increase both military expenditures and its area of control. Simply put, the more resources the Japanese controlled, the more they needed. This was a problem the Japanese never solved.

Most people know at least a little bit about the Japanese attack on Pearl Harbor on December 7th, 1941 (December 8th in Japan). What led to Japan's decision to attack the United States? In September 1940, the Japanese, Germans, and Italians signed the Tripartite Pact (sometimes referred to by those three powers as the Pact of Steel or the Anti-Comintern Pact, with the Comintern being the organization of worldwide communist parties run by Joseph Stalin). Almost immediately thereafter, the Japanese invaded French Indochina, today known as Vietnam.

France had been defeated by Hitler in June 1940, and Hitler expressed his desire to "give" Indochina to the Japanese. The collaborationist Vichy government of France agreed, and on September 27th, 1940, Japan entered the French colony. The Japanese occupation of Vietnam was initially planned to halt the flow of weapons into southern China coming through Vietnam's northern border. But eventually, the Japanese moved to take the whole country, though many French administrators and policemen took orders from them. The Japanese believed they could seize the rice and rubber produced in Vietnam (Japan's food production was not keeping up with its population growth, and rubber was needed in military equipment) and use its ports as a springboard for future military moves, specifically the Dutch East Indies, a petroleum-rich territory.

The United States had been closely aligned with France before the war, and after the French defeat, it remained close to France's government-in-exile. Though there was no formal alliance between the US and the French, the seizure of French territory showed that the Japanese were working in concert with Hitler to a degree. Since the end of World War One, the United States had become increasingly isolationist. Many in the country believed that WWI, which had been presented to the public as the "war to end all wars," had been fought for nothing—the world had not changed, and 100,000 American soldiers had died in nine months for another war to break out just twenty years later.

However, by 1940, the American outlook had begun to change. The US relationship with China was both interesting and complicated. For many reasons, America was viewed in a more positive light by the Chinese. In early 1940, the famous volunteer American pilots, the Flying Tigers, began to fight against the Japanese, and a number of former American military men were hired or volunteered as advisers to the Chinese military (this later included the Communist armed forces as well). Japanese atrocities had also been reported on, and new ones seemed to occur every day. This enraged greater and greater numbers of Americans as late 1941 approached.

The last straw for the Japanese was when US president Franklin Delano Roosevelt announced a total freeze of Japanese assets in the United States, along with an embargo on airplanes, parts, machine tools, and aviation gasoline in July 1941. Oil, iron, and steel scrap followed. (Old New York subway cars, among other things, had been scrapped and sent to Japan, where the recycled steel was used to build warships.) Other commodities, such as wheat, rice, and other agricultural goods, were also on the American list of embargoed goods. With the announcement of the embargo, Roosevelt demanded the withdrawal of Japanese troops and talks on the withdrawal of Japanese troops from China.

Neither was going to happen. The Japanese had spent much money and many lives to seize their new empire. Japanese society had been transformed into a militaristic police state to further its imperial goals. The Japanese secret police, a branch of the military, was called the *Kempeitai* ("thought police"), and it rivaled the Gestapo in its brutality. Reversing this would likely deal a huge blow to the military power at home and result in the Japanese nation "losing face."

Although the Japanese rejected the Americans' demands, they agreed to talks in Washington to see if the United States and Japan could reach some sort of agreement or compromise. These talks were going on as the Japanese fleet sailed toward Pearl Harbor. On December 6ᵗʰ, Roosevelt cabled a letter to "His Imperial Majesty, the Emperor of Japan," in which he wrote, in part, "During the past few weeks it has become clear to the world that Japanese military, naval and air forces have been sent to Southern Indo-China in such large numbers as to create a reasonable doubt on the part of other nations that this continuing concentration in Indochina is not defensive in its character ... I address myself to Your Majesty at this moment in the fervent hope that Your Majesty may, as I am doing, give thought in this definite emergency to ways of dispelling the dark clouds. I am confident that both of us, for the sake of the peoples not only of our own great countries but for the sake of humanity in neighboring territories, have a sacred duty to restore traditional amity and prevent further death and destruction in the world."

The Japanese response came the next morning.

Chapter 6 – WWII and Late Showa Japan

The answer to President Roosevelt's letter to the emperor came in the form of the Japanese fleet's air arm on the morning of December 7ᵗʰ, 1941, with the infamous attack on Pearl Harbor, the naval base of the United States Pacific Fleet. The main Japanese fleet left the Kuril Islands off the far northern coast of Japan (they are now controlled by Russia) on November 26ᵗʰ.

The main target of the Japanese was America's aircraft carriers, the *Enterprise*, *Saratoga*, and *Lexington*. Japan's strategic and tactical thinking was ahead of the United States at the time. Those at the top of the Imperial Japanese Navy understood the value of the aircraft carriers in a way many of their counterparts in the US Navy did not. That is not to say that many American naval officers did not value the carriers; many of them believed that the "flat-tops" would be the key to any war in the Pacific. However, many of the top commanders were set in their ways, having risen through the ranks in another era. Many still believed that the battleships and their powerful guns would be the key weapon in any Pacific war.

Very few believed that after Pearl Harbor happened. The bomber range of aircraft in those days was measured in hundreds of miles. The range of the most powerful battleships was maybe twenty miles. The math was clear, yet old ideas die hard. On the evening of December 7ᵗʰ in Hawaii, Americans realized three things: they had seriously underestimated Japan and its military, they were fortunate that the three American carriers were not at Pearl Harbor that morning, and the US had better start building carriers—fast.

The damage inflicted at Pearl Harbor is well known, as was the shock of the surprise attack. Americans listening to President Roosevelt's radio broadcast heard the famous opening, "Yesterday, December 7th, 1941, a date which will live in infamy, the United States of America was suddenly and deliberately attacked by naval and air forces of the Empire of Japan." They also heard the president tell them of heavy losses and that the Japanese had attacked American and British forces throughout the Pacific. "I regret to tell you that very many American lives have been lost. In addition American ships have been reported torpedoed on the high seas between San Francisco and Honolulu. Yesterday the Japanese Government also launched an attack against Malaya. Last night Japanese forces attacked Hong Kong. Last night Japanese forces attacked Guam. Last night Japanese forces attacked the Philippine Islands. Last night the Japanese attacked Wake Island. And this morning the Japanese attacked Midway Island." He closed by asking (and receiving) Congress's declaration of war against Japan.

If you look back on WWII in the Pacific, it seems inevitable that the United States would have won the war. The population of the US was double that of Japan. Americans had greater resources of all kinds, and it was the greatest industrial power in the world. The Japanese were going to face the power of the United States alone. Many in Japan realized it was a one-sided match, though the Japanese cause was helped to a degree when Germany declared war on the US in support of its Japanese ally.

Still, one man believed the fight against the Americans would be an uphill battle, one that Japan was unlikely to win if the war lasted a long time. This man was the planner of the Pearl Harbor attack, the commander of the fleet that sailed toward Hawaii, and one of the architects of both the modern Japanese navy and its initial strategy. He was Admiral Isoroku Yamamoto, and he had both lived and toured the United States in the 1920s. Yamamoto had met with his naval counterparts from all over the Western world at various diplomatic functions and talks.

Illustration 20: Yamamoto in 1940. In his essay on Yamamoto, Australian commentator Clive James said, "His is the face of a man who knows he will lose, but will fight you anyway."
https://en.wikipedia.org/wiki/File:Portrait_of_Yamamoto_Isoroku.jpg

Yamamoto had been a mover and shaker in the Japanese military for quite some time. However, his opinions were not popular at the top levels of either the army or the navy and especially not with General Hideki Tojo, the man who would become prime minister in October 1941. Tojo and Yamamoto did not like each other, and their opinions regarding Japanese expansion differed greatly. Yamamoto felt the Japanese invasion of Manchuria was a mistake and brought about by insubordinate officers operating as their own private army (which they were). Tojo eventually supported the Manchurian invasion, though he, too, was taken by surprise by the Kwantung Army's independence.

Yamamoto also opposed the invasion of China and the navy's role in it. He believed that Japan could get much of what it wanted from using its navy in a punitive role, backing up Japanese claims and security with naval shells. As a navy man, Yamamoto was insulted by the army's use and opinion of the navy as a ferrying service for ground troops back and forth from Japan to China. He also believed Japan would get bogged down in China unless the militarists were removed from power. If they weren't, Japanese troops would be fighting in China for years to come, something Yamamoto believed they could not win.

These opinions cost Yamamoto dearly in the early and mid-1930s. He was essentially exiled internally for a time and given a cushy but unimportant post away from Tokyo. He also received many death threats for his opinions on the war and future wars. There was one thing the government could not really do, though, and that was dismiss Yamamoto. He was far too popular with the sailors in the navy, as he knew what he was doing, cared about them, and stood up for them.

It should be said that Yamamoto was no peace-loving "dove." He believed that Japan's armed forces should play an important role in the country, and he was not against using them if he believed in the cause. Yamamoto was a Japanese warrior; even if he believed the war was a losing proposition, he would not only follow orders but also give his all to do what he believed might be impossible.

Though many at the top disliked Yamamoto personally, most recognized his brilliance. He was appointed admiral in late 1940 and given the task of developing the plans for an attack against the United States. As commander of the effort, Yamamoto reviewed the quality of pilots, their aircraft, the maintenance and building of ships, and much else. Though the Japanese fleet was advanced in 1940, it is said that Yamamoto injected an energy into it that had been lacking before his arrival. He also emphasized that the Imperial Japanese Navy (IJN) would be the crucial branch of the military in any upcoming conflict in the Pacific. Yamamoto's and his tactical success at Pearl Harbor exacerbated the conflict that had slowly begun to rise between the army and the navy. Later in the war, the conflict became an impediment to a unified Japanese war plan.

Yamamoto has two famous quotes about the United States and the possibility of Japan going to war with it. The first one was edited to make it seem like Yamamoto was in line with the general Japanese military opinion. Unfortunately for the Japanese, many of their top commanders in both branches believed that if the US was hit hard enough, it would sue for peace. The Japanese believed its government and people were divided, weakened by the Great Depression, and soft because of their "decadent" lifestyle (jazz, booze, girls, gangsters, etc.). Yamamoto's quote reflects the opposite opinion, though the last line was removed to make it seem as if the admiral was calling for an all-out war with the US:

"Should hostilities once break out between Japan and the United States, it would not be enough that we take Guam and the Philippines, nor even Hawaii and San Francisco. To make victory certain, we would have to march into Washington and dictate the terms of peace in the White House. I wonder if our politicians [who speak so lightly of a Japanese-American war] have confidence as to the final outcome and are prepared to make the necessary sacrifices."

When the quote was discovered by the United States, it was used in its altered form for propaganda, indicating to Americans that the Japanese had intentions far beyond the Pacific.

Still, Yamamoto was a soldier. He followed orders and planned not only for the attack on Pearl Harbor but also for the entire Japanese campaign in the Pacific, which would be launched at the same time. If he was given an order to attack, he would, and he would try to give Japan the best chance of victory. Still, underlying all of the planning was nagging doubts. These doubts were made quite clear in this quote: "In the first six to twelve months of a war with the United States and Great Britain I will run wild and win victory upon victory. But then, if the war continues after that, I have no expectation of success."

After the news of Pearl Harbor hit Japan, there was great rejoicing. Many felt the war was all but won and that it was only a matter of time before the US would sue for peace. Yamamoto had spent considerable time in America. He went to college for a year there and had friends in the United States, including military men, government men, and journalists. He had toured the country and seen its factories. In response to the cheering in the streets about Pearl Harbor, he privately let his feelings known to his inner circle:

"A military man can scarcely pride himself on having 'smitten a sleeping enemy'; it is more a matter of shame, simply, for the one smitten. I would rather you made your appraisal after seeing what the enemy does, since it is certain that, angered and outraged, he will soon launch a determined counterattack."

The admiral was not happy about the rejoicing in Japan over Pearl Harbor or what he saw as its failure. "The mindless rejoicing at home is really appalling; it makes me fear that the first blow against Tokyo will make them wilt at once ... I only wish that [the Americans] had also had, say, three carriers at Hawaii." And, of course, there is his most famous quote: "I fear all we have done is to awaken a sleeping giant and fill him with a terrible resolve."

In the end, Yamamoto was right, and with hindsight, we know Japan did not stand a chance, not with the riches and agricultural, industrial, and scientific power of the United States. However, Yamamoto was right about running roughshod throughout the Far East. Within months, the Japanese Empire spanned a significant portion of the Asian mainland and much of the Pacific.

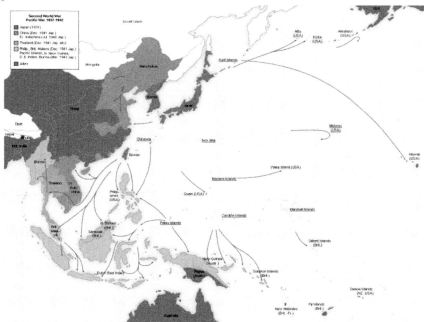

Illustration 21: The Japanese Empire at its greatest extent, 1941 to mid-1942.
*User:San Jose, This file is licensed under the Creative Commons Attribution-Share Alike 3.0 Unported license;<https://creativecommons.org/licenses/by-sa/3.0/deed.en >
https://en.wikipedia.org/wiki/File:Second_world_war_asia_1937-1942_map_en6.png*

Pearl Harbor was not the only surprise for the Western powers. The British believed their armies and positions in their colonies of Malaya (today's Malaysia) and Singapore (at the tip of the Malaysian Peninsula) were impregnable. However, another soon-to-be-famous Japanese general, Tomoyuki Yamashita, led his troops in an amazingly mobile campaign (considering the extremely heavy jungle and poor roads) down the Malay Peninsula. Japanese forces under Yamashita repeatedly outmaneuvered and outflanked the stunned British, who retreated to what they thought was an island fortress, the city of Singapore.

The problem with the defense of Singapore is that it was focused on meeting an attack from the sea. The coastal guns protecting the city from a seaborne invasion would not turn 180 degrees to fire upon an attack from the rear, and the British did not have any significant defenses between the city itself and the Malay Peninsula on the other side of the island. They believed that the marshes and virtually roadless approaches to the city from the rear were impossible for a sizable force to navigate. They were wrong. Even before the attack, Yamashita and other Japanese officers had reports and photographs about the lack of defenses on the north side of the city. The Battle of Singapore lasted a week, from February 8th to February 15th, 1942, ending in what British Prime Minister Churchill called the "greatest military defeat in British history."

The image of General Yamashita demanding the formal surrender from the unfortunately timid-looking British General Arthur Percival became one of the best known of the war. In Japan, it was celebrated. In Great Britain, it was a humiliation, and in the United States, it was motivation.

Illustration 22: Yamashita seated, center facing camera. The British believed they were in negotiations; the Japanese demanded unconditional surrender.
https://en.wikipedia.org/wiki/File:BritishSurrender.jpg

At the same time Yamashita was waging his campaign in Malaysia and Singapore, other Japanese forces were fighting American and Filipino forces in the Philippines to the north. The Philippines was under American control, having been seized from Spain in the Spanish-American War of 1898. The Philippines was resource-rich, though not in vital petroleum, and seen by the Japanese as a threat to their campaign in China and, ultimately, to Japan itself.

The Great East Asia Co-prosperity Sphere

It's important to remember that for many of the native people of Asia (the Vietnamese and others who lived in Indochina, the people of the Philippines, the Malay Peninsula, and Indonesia in particular), being a possession or colony of a Western power was not what many people wanted. In the Philippines, the United States fought a brutal war against Filipino guerrillas from 1899 to 1902. Though the United States gave the Filipinos their independence in 1946 (a date that had been chosen before the war), quite a number of Filipinos believed the Japanese were there to throw off the yoke of Western/white imperialism.

This was partially due to clever Japanese propaganda, though the idea behind it started long before the racially-biased military government took power in the 1930s. Japanese intellectuals in the later Meiji period believed that if Japan became strong enough, it might unite the people of Asia against the Western powers and be the axis of power in Asia. However, by the late 1930s, this idea had become less and less about the other people of Asia and more about Japan being the axis of power. The Japanese were able to convince a number of influential people in India and the Philippines that Japanese rule would be benevolent and good for their countries. To help convince the people of the newly conquered territories of their intentions, the Japanese developed the idea of the Greater East Asia Co-prosperity Sphere, which depicted the Japanese as just one of many nations in Asia determined to forge a way to a bright future with Asia in mind.

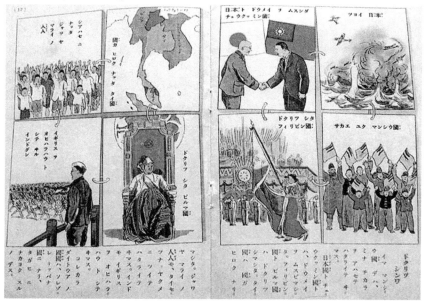

Illustration 23: Page from propaganda booklet heralding the Greater East Asia Co-prosperity Sphere. Collaborationist leaders in conquered territories are seen making friends with the Japanese.
https://en.wikipedia.org/wiki/File:Japanese_1943_propaganda_booklet_2.JPG

Except for the people at the very top of the food chain who enriched themselves during the Japanese occupation, most people in the territories conquered by Japan came to quickly realize that the idea of a benevolent Japanese occupation was complete fiction.

Hundreds of thousands of people in the Pacific died from Japanese action in the form of massacres and deaths during imprisonment. More died from starvation and disease. Hundreds of thousands of women, from Korea to China to Malaysia, were forced into sexual slavery for the pleasure of Japanese troops, and many did not survive the war. To this day, the treatment of "comfort women" is still a political sticking point between Japan and the countries it subjugated.

The Philippines

Many people in the United States believed that the Americans would easily defeat the Japanese in a fair fight. However, the surrender of the final American outpost in the Philippines—the island of Corregidor in Manila Bay on May 8th, 1942—and the evacuation of the American governor and military commander Douglas MacArthur caused many Americans to wake up and realize that the war against Japan was going to take much longer than they had anticipated.

The Americans were given ample motivation for revenge when the treatment of US and Filipino prisoners of war and American civilians began to filter into the news. The same treatment and the same reaction occurred in Great Britain, Australia, New Zealand, Canada, and India when news of the treatment of their soldiers and civilians made the papers. The same held true for the Dutch, whose considerable navy in the Pacific was placed under American command for the war.

The horrors that Allied prisoners of war faced at the hands of the Japanese rival some of the cruelest tales from Nazi-occupied Europe. In the Philippines, Americans who had surrendered were marched some seventy miles down the Bataan Peninsula on the opposite side of Manila Bay from the Philippine capital. The tales of brutality are horrifying. Men were buried alive. Soldiers were tortured until they killed others. There were hundreds of deaths from thirst and wounds. Mass beheadings and shootings took place.

Some of the pictures were captured in Japanese papers and publicized back in the US. A number of escapees also made it safely to Allied territory and told the grim tales of what was happening to thousands upon thousands of prisoners. The Bataan Death March became a rallying cry for America. To be quite frank, it built up a tremendous desire for revenge on American soldiers, sailors, airmen, and Marines fighting across the Pacific. The treatment of prisoners in the Philippines became a rallying cry, and the war in the Pacific quickly became one of racial brutality.

Illustration 24: American poster emphasizing the treatment of US prisoners of war and what was expected to avenge them.
Public image, courtesy of the US Department of the Treasury;
https://en.wikipedia.org/wiki/File:Anti-Japan2.png

The Japanese had their own violent propaganda. One famous poster depicts Japan sending the American and British fleets to the bottom of the sea by a powerful samurai, which appealed to the Japanese people's sense of history and glory.

Illustration 25: An example of Japanese propaganda during the war.
https://commons.wikimedia.org/wiki/File:Farewell,_American_Soldiers!.jpg

Yamamoto did indeed run roughshod all over the Pacific. Australia was threatened, and its northern city of Darwin was bombed by Japanese planes, setting off a case of invasion hysteria for a brief time. With the exception of British troops in Malaya, India, and Burma, which would make up yet another front of the war from late 1942 to 1945, the British had been driven from Asia. The large Dutch colony that is today Indonesia was conquered in 1942, with the future president of independent Indonesia, Sukarno, heading a collaborationist government for the Japanese. Indonesia was the main prize for Japan since it was (and still is) one of the world's major oil producers, but Indonesia could not be held without conquering the territories around it.

The Americans had been pushed back. The most important of their Pacific possessions, the Philippines, was completely occupied, though hardly subdued, for a fierce insurgency emerged on many of the islands that both fought the Japanese and supplied intelligence. American possessions were overrun, including Wake Island, American Samoa, Guam, and more. The Japanese even invaded the Alaskan Aleutian Islands of Attu and Kiska, though this was a halfhearted effort that was easily repelled by the United States.

In Japan, most people rejoiced. Japan's victories proved to many that the Japanese were just as capable, if not more capable, of doing what the Western powers had done for years: conquer territory. Unfortunately for the Japanese people, many of their leaders believed that it was only a matter of time before the US asked to negotiate. The United States was struck hard and demoralized by the attacks on Pearl Harbor and other American possessions. Hitler's declaration of war on the United States meant that the Americans would be fighting a war against two of the greatest powers in the world. To the Japanese, it seemed inevitable that the Americans would have to sue for peace.

That illusion ended rather quickly. On April 18th, 1942, American bombers dropped bombs on Tokyo and Yokohama, Tokyo's port. The actual damage caused by the Doolittle Raid (named for the US Air Force general who commanded the effort) was minimal, but the feeling of security the Japanese had felt since December 7th, 1941, was shattered. Many people who had private doubts about the wisdom of attacking the US now saw their doubts confirmed.

In early June 1942, the Japanese launched what they hoped was another surprise attack against the Americans. This time, the attack came at Midway Island, west of Hawaii. The attack came as no surprise, for the Americans had broken the Japanese naval code, which carried the orders to assault the island by air, soften its defenses, and land an amphibious force. The battle was a disaster for the Japanese. Due to a combination of skill, luck, and tenacity, the Americans, though outnumbered, destroyed the bulk of Japan's carrier fleet in one fell swoop. In addition to 4 sunken fleet carriers, nearly 250 Japanese planes were shot down, as well as many of the nation's best pilots. Many on both sides of the Pacific realized that Midway could be the turning point in the Pacific War.

One of those was Admiral Yamamoto, who now realized that his time of "running roughshod" over the Americans was over. Though a Japanese offensive was beginning on the island of Guadalcanal in the Solomon Islands, from the Battle of Midway forward, the Japanese would essentially be on the defensive for the rest of the war.

The story of the war in the Pacific is long and brutal. The Japanese perversion of the samurai code, backed up by severe training and indoctrination, led many Japanese defensive efforts in the Pacific to be fought to the last man or close to it. American troops learned the hard way that many Japanese offering themselves up as prisoners of war were often hiding grenades, knives, or other explosive charges on their person when attempting to surrender. When American troops approached, Japanese soldiers would either attack or blow themselves up. Soon, any Japanese that appeared to be surrendering was ordered to strip naked to assure he was not carrying anything on his person. On many occasions, Japanese troops attempting to really give themselves up were killed by their comrades as traitors to the emperor. Honestly, many Japanese were also killed by American and other Allied troops when they attempted to give up or when they refused an offer of surrender.

Japanese officers and men were told that the "bushido spirit" of the Japanese would win the day. Like Hitler in the waning days of his empire, the Japanese were told that their own personal will guided by the bushido spirit of the samurai would result in victory even if the enemy was better armed and numerically superior. One result of this was the infamous banzai attacks. ("banzai" was a shortening of the war cry "Tennoheika Banzai," which means "Long Live the Emperor.") Banzai attacks took place throughout the war. Groups, sometimes numbering up to four thousand men, would charge enemy positions in a human wave. The hope was that enough soldiers would survive to break through the line of terrified defenders and reverse the tide of battle. Though largely ineffective and wasteful, banzai attacks could indeed be terrifying, especially to fresh American troops. Their terror increased when the attack came at night, which they frequently did.

By the latter part of the war, many American soldiers strangely hoped for a banzai attack since mowing down hundreds of Japanese was far easier than digging them out of the thousands of concrete bunkers and fortified caves they retreated into as the Americans advanced closer to Japan itself.

The battles that led Allied forces to Japan's doorstep in the spring/summer of 1945 are so famous and covered in thousands of books, including Captivating History's various offerings on the war.

These battles include Guadalcanal, New Guinea, Tarawa, Peleliu, Saipan, Iwo Jima, and Okinawa, just to name seven. As the Allies, led by the Americans, pushed toward Japan, Japanese tactics changed. After the first few battles and immediately after Guadalcanal, the Japanese were mainly on the defensive.

Though the island of Peleliu was not inhabited by Japanese civilians, the battle there, which took place from September to November 1944, marked the shift in Japanese tactics. In cave after cave on the island's mountainous spine, US Marines blew up, shot, and burned Japanese defenders who refused to surrender. Others were effectively buried alive by explosive charges coming not only from the Marines but also American air power and massive naval bombardments.

Large numbers of civilians lived on the islands of Saipan and Okinawa, which were both Japanese possessions before the war. In some cases, the traditional Japanese mindset of suicide before dishonor caused civilians to kill themselves rather than surrender to the Americans. This mindset, combined with tales told in school and in the media of how Americans would rape and kill all Japanese women and even eat babies, also prompted civilians to kill themselves. Japanese-American translators spoke to them from American lines, assuring them of good treatment, which the vast majority who did surrender received, but this tactic did not always work. Those who wished to surrender were often holed up with Japanese soldiers, who threatened to kill them if they tried. Many civilians were killed when soldiers blew up their own positions rather than give up.

On Saipan, hundreds of Japanese civilians, most of them women, the elderly, and children, jumped off the now famous "Suicide Cliffs," despite the entreaties of American troops and other Japanese who had successfully given up. Famous newsreels of the incident show Japanese mothers carrying babies in their arms as they jumped off the steep cliffs into the sea. This type of behavior continued in Okinawa, where, on occasion, civilians would be forced to wear explosive charges and attempt to surrender to the Americans, only to be blown up by Japanese officers controlling the detonator. Confronted with this type of resistance, American soldiers, officials, civilians, and politicians all dreaded the idea of an eventual invasion of the Japanese Home Islands.

The war continued at sea as well. To make a success of their "island-hopping" strategy in the Pacific, the Americans needed to establish control of the air and sea leading to, around, and on their next target. Great naval battles, most of which were American victories (the Battle of Savo Island off the coast of Guadalcanal was the biggest US defeat at sea), continued until 1945, though by that time, they mostly consisted of the Japanese using their famous kamikaze tactics from the air.

The last true gasp of the Imperial Japanese Navy came at the Battle of Leyte Gulf during the American return to the Philippines, led by General Douglas MacArthur, which took place in late October 1944. It could have ended in a significant Japanese victory on both sea and land if not for the brave actions of a handful of American sailors, a motley assortment of destroyer escorts, and Japanese timidity caused by miscalculation and the desire to avoid heavy losses.

Though most would not admit it, some Japanese had come to believe that Yamamoto had been right. (American pilots, guided by intelligence from code-breakers, shot down the transport aircraft carrying Yamamoto over the Solomon Islands in late 1943.) Still, despite mounting losses, the Japanese military refused to acknowledge what was fast becoming the inevitable. And remember, the United States was fighting a two-front war. Despite having given priority to defeating Germany, it still deployed greater numbers of ships, planes, men, ammunition, and every type of war-making material than Japan. At the end of the wars, just *one part* of the entire US Pacific Fleet, the Seventh Fleet, was bigger than all the other navies in the world at the time—*combined.*

US naval production July 1940–August 1945: 74,896 ships, including 10 battleships, 27 aircraft carriers, and 111 escort carriers.

Japan naval production, including warships built before the war with America began: 650.[1]

---

[1] According to *Oxford Companion to World War II* and *Kaigun: Strategy, Tactics, and Technology in the Imperial Japanese Navy, 1887-1941*

The disparity in aircraft production was similar, and the Japanese never developed the heavy long-range bombers that the Americans used to such great effect from early 1944 onward in their campaign to destroy Japan's war-making capacity and morale. One last fact: it's been estimated that every American soldier or Marine in the Pacific carried or had access to one ton of supplies for each man. The Japanese soldier had access to less than one hundred pounds.

One of the reasons for the disparity in supplies, other than the United States' incredible industrial capacity, was that the Japanese needed to bring most of their supplies, including vital resources like oil, rubber, and iron, to the Home Islands. The Americans had everything they needed at home and the industrial capacity to convert resources to war materiel. Making things even worse for the Japanese was that by early 1945, the Japanese merchant fleet essentially ceased to exist. The prime reason for this, among many, was the success of the US submarine fleet, which by the end of the war was literally sinking wooden sailboats laden with small amounts of supplies with their deck guns.

If that wasn't bad enough, the American strategic bombing campaign, whose eligibility as a war crime has been discussed in both Japan and in some quarters of the US since the end of the war, destroyed virtually every Japanese city of any importance to the war effort. Just one raid, which took place in one night, by American B-29 *Superfortress* on March 9th/10th, 1945, killed an estimated 100,000 people. Japanese cities at the time were still largely made of wood, and the resulting fires reached temperatures as high as 1,000°F.

Despite all of this, the Japanese government refused to surrender, even after Japan's island of Okinawa was captured, just under one thousand miles south of Tokyo. The Battle of Okinawa, which lasted from April to late June 1945, put the famous kamikaze pilots in the history books. Somewhere in the neighborhood of three thousand planes of all kinds were launched as suicide bombs at American ships offshore. The campaign did not change the outcome of the war and likely did not even delay it. A small number of US ships were sunk, and hundreds were damaged by these men who believed there was no greater honor than "dying for the emperor."

As the Americans approached, the Japanese government introduced mass conscription and was said to have issued weapons, largely in the form of wooden stakes, to a million people for the defense of their homeland. American military estimates put potential Allied casualties of a successful invasion of Japan at a million or more. Estimates of Japanese civilian casualties were put in the millions.

The Bomb

"If they do not accept our terms, they can expect a rain of ruin from the air, the like of which has never been seen on this earth."

With that statement, which was seen and heard by millions of Americans on newsreels and the radio and read by additional millions in the paper, President Harry Truman made it clear that the US intended to bomb Japan into submission. Knowing now what people did not know then, Truman was referencing the potential use of America's secret weapon: the atomic bomb. However, given the destructive power of the American firebombing campaign, neither the Japanese nor anyone else outside the relatively few people who knew about the bomb believed what Truman spoke about would be so monumentally different and change the world forever.

On July 26th, 1945, the Big Three—the leaders of the US, the Soviet Union, and Great Britain—issued the Potsdam Declaration to the world and, specifically, to Japan. Much of the declaration dealt with the Allies' intentions for Japan after its surrender. It emphasized the establishment of a democratic government and justice for war criminals. The Allies also expressed they had no desire for vengeance on the Japanese people "as a race." The ominous part came at the end:

"We call upon the government of Japan to proclaim now the unconditional surrender of all Japanese armed forces, and to provide proper and adequate assurances of their good faith in such action. The alternative for Japan is prompt and utter destruction."

Within the Japanese government, there was division. At the highest levels of the civilian government, the consensus was that Japan had no choice but that the question of the post-war role of the emperor needed clarification. Feelers would have to be sent out to the USSR in the hopes that Stalin would play the role of mediator between the US and Japan.

Among the military leadership (General Tojo had been dismissed from his military position and the post of prime minister in September 1944), there were two opinions. 1) The ultimatum was dishonorable and should be rejected openly. 2) It should be accepted, but the question about the emperor needed clarification. A message went out to the Soviet Union about Japan's thoughts on the matter. There was no reply from Stalin. No message whatsoever was sent to the United States.

There was a fundamental lack of understanding of the Americans by the Japanese. Generally speaking, in Japanese negotiations, an open and clear rejection is thought of in two ways. First, it ends the negotiations or the possibility of them. And second, it sends a strong message of disrespect. When no reply is given, it could also mean two things: "We are waiting for better terms or clarification and do not wish to commit ourselves until then." or "We reject the offer (or demand, in this case) and wait for another." In the United States, no answer was a rejection. And after Pearl Harbor, Bataan, tens of thousands of dead and wounded, the expense, and much else, the US was not suited for patience.

The details of the debate within the US government and military as to whether or not to drop the bomb are best explained in another book since this is just an introductory guide. Suffice it to say, Truman decided that the bomb should be dropped. The US military had chosen the historic port city of Hiroshima, which was relatively undamaged at this point in the war, as the first target.

On August 6th, 1945, the atomic bomb called "Little Boy" was dropped on Hiroshima. It exploded about two thousand feet above the center of the city, and within a fraction of a second, the temperature in Hiroshima exceeded *seven thousand degrees.* Within a second, some seventy thousand people were killed, many of them leaving no trace except a reverse shadow that had indicated their existence. Over the next weeks and months, another 100,000 people would die from the effects of the blast.

Illustration 26: The mushroom cloud at Hiroshima moments after the blast taken from ten kilometers away.

https://en.wikipedia.org/wiki/File:Hiroshima_10km.jpg

After the bomb on Hiroshima had been dropped, there was debate within the Japanese government. At a meeting of the Supreme War Council, which included both military and civilians, four conditions for the surrender of Japan were developed. They were the retention of the emperor, disarmament, that Japan would deal with war criminals, and that there would be no occupation of Japan. To this day, it is hard to imagine the mindset of the Japanese leadership, especially after reports of what had just happened in Hiroshima filtered into Tokyo. Once again, it seemed as if the Japanese were in a time warp. They existed in a world before August 6th, but the United States and its allies were in a completely new one that included the possibility of the total annihilation of Japan in moments.

On August 9th, Truman ordered the use of the second and more powerful bomb, "Fat Man." At 11:02 a.m., Fat Man, a plutonium bomb (Little Boy's was a uranium bomb), detonated over Nagasaki, another southern port city and military installation. Due to the geography of the city, which helped contain the blast and its effects to a certain extent, the casualties at Nagasaki were less than that of Hiroshima, though still monumental. Estimates of immediate deaths in Nagasaki run from twenty thousand to seventy-five thousand or more. Like Hiroshima, tens of thousands would die in the next weeks and months from radiation poisoning, succumbing to infection of wounds, lack of proper medical care, and more.

Illustration 27: What was left of the center of Nagasaki after the blast.
https://en.wikipedia.org/wiki/File:Nagasaki_temple_destroyed.jpg

No one is exactly sure how many more survivors of the blasts (called *hibakusha*, meaning "person affected by a bomb" or "person affected by radiation from a bomb") died from sickness brought on by their exposure to radiation. Estimates range from the thousands to the tens of thousands. Only one man (despite claims from about seventy others), Tsutomu Yamaguchi, is recognized as having survived *both* nuclear explosions. He had been stationed in Hiroshima and fled to Nagasaki to be with his wife and children when the second bomb was dropped. Yamaguchi died in 2010.

After the Nagasaki blast, it was clear even to those at the top that Japan had better surrender or face literal extinction. Even so, debates continued as to how to go about it. Eventually, Hirohito took matters into his own hands. On August 15th, 1945, Hirohito did something that no Japanese emperor ever had—he addressed the nation in his own voice. In a radio broadcast, Hirohito told the Japanese that they needed to be prepared to "bear the unbearable," by which he meant defeat and occupation. His speech also contained a controversial phrase that has been used ever since by far-right Japanese nationalists to "prove" that Japan did not really lose the war: "The gallant fighting of military and naval forces, the diligence and assiduity of Our servants of the State and the devoted service of Our one hundred million people, the war situation has developed *not necessarily to Japan's advantage, while the general trends of the world have all turned against her interest* [italics author's emphasis]."

The delay between the blast at Nagasaki and the emperor's speech was due in large part to a series of attempted coup d'états in which younger and lower-ranking officers attempted to overthrow the government, take the emperor hostage, and continue the war. Through force and guile, cooler heads prevailed, and the Japanese averted complete obliteration.

The question of whether or not the United States should have dropped the atomic bombs has raged since 1945. To this day, many in Japan believe that the dropping of the bombs should be considered a war crime. Many Americans believe it saved American and Japanese lives since an invasion of the islands would have been launched if the bombs were not dropped. In a CBS News "Victory in the Pacific" special that aired in 1995, one *hibakusha* said that he had a message for his countrymen: "That Japan was working on the bomb, and would have used it if they had developed it first, what do you think about that?"

On the day of the Nagasaki explosion, the Soviet Union attacked the large Japanese army in China and Manchuria, rapidly driving them backward and eventually liberating much of what Japan had conquered. The areas of southern Japan and Indochina still under Japanese control when the surrender was signed on September 2nd, 1945, were slowly repatriated to their decimated countries over the next few months. The Soviets occupied the Japanese Kurile Islands, which was north of the country (Russia still holds it to this day), and the northern half of Sakhalin Island, just north of the Japanese island of Hokkaido.

"These proceedings are at an end."

Those were the words spoken by General Douglas MacArthur on the deck of the battleship USS *Missouri* on September 2nd, 1945. It was docked in Tokyo Bay for the formal ceremony of Japan's surrender. In all aspects but one, Japan surrendered unconditionally. The one condition? That the emperor remained as head of state. This was agreed to by the Americans, not because they had to but because they knew with the retention of Hirohito and his cooperation, their occupation of Japan, which began even before the surrender ceremony, would be smoother and more peaceful. However, the Americans did have one condition for the emperor: renounce the idea that he or any emperor to come was divine. Hirohito had no choice in the matter.

Illustration 28: Japanese officials surrender on the USS Missouri, September 2nd, 1945.
https://commons.wikimedia.org/wiki/File:Surrender_of_Japan_-_USS_Missouri.jpg

With the surrender of Japan, WWII had come to an end. Japan once again would set about astounding the world in its capacity to rebuild itself in the years to come.

Chapter 7 – The Showa Era, Part II

Illustration 29: The most famous post-war Japanese "product," Godzilla, has his own star on the Hollywood Walk of Fame!

This file is licensed under the Creative Commons Attribution-Share Alike 2.0 Generic license; https://creativecommons.org/licenses/by-sa/2.0/ https://en.wikipedia.org/wiki/File:Godzillastar.jpg

Japan lost about three million people during the war. Most of those were military personnel. Despite the intense bombing of Japanese cities and the two atomic explosions, civilian losses were much less than those of Germany and the Soviet Union, both of which had been invaded by enemy troops. The Japanese were about to be occupied by the US, but the nature of that occupation was still unknown. The tales of American plans to rape and murder that had spread during the war were still rife, and many Japanese expected a reign of terror. The emperor's words did help to calm and steady the nation in the face of the unknown.

In actuality, the face of the American occupation was well known to the Japanese, for he had been one of their foremost enemies during the war: General of the Army Douglas MacArthur. MacArthur had been in charge of US ground forces in the drive toward Japan. Along with naval commander Admiral Chester Nimitz, he had organized forces in the largest theater of the war for one aim: to defeat and possibly destroy Japan.

Truman had appointed MacArthur for a number of reasons, the most important one being that MacArthur was supremely qualified for the job. He had commanded and coordinated one of the most complicated military campaigns in history, and his experience as governor of the Philippines (which did, according to the agreement with the US, gain their independence in 1946) gave him the administrative skills he would need to govern Japan.

MacArthur was also supremely confident in himself—many said to the point of arrogance—but he backed his arrogance up with skill, determination, and foresight. Truman was also a bit wary of MacArthur's ambition, for rumors circulated in Washington that the popular general was interested in running for president, and there was an election coming in 1948 that Truman intended to win. Keeping MacArthur busy thousands of miles away was a political move, though that was secondary to Truman's assessment of the general's ability.

One thing was made very clear to Emperor Hirohito: MacArthur was in charge. The general would discuss, usually with the emperor's aides, what was being done and what was being planned. It was made clear in their first meeting that the emperor's role was to keep the Japanese people calm and focused on rebuilding. The emperor and what was left of the Japanese government would actively work to make sure that no resistance to the occupation was mounted. Hirohito would also endorse, or at least not condemn, MacArthur's plans for governing Japan and restructuring its government into a truly democratic one.

In return, the emperor would enjoy the life in the Imperial Palace that he had always enjoyed, and he would have ample time to continue his study of botany. Should the emperor not comply, and honestly there was no real question that he wouldn't, he would be completely sidelined and isolated. The position of emperor might even be written out of the new Japanese constitution if he refused to cooperate. The constitution was being worked on by MacArthur and his staff even before the occupation began.

Illustration 30: MacArthur and Hirohito, September 1945. This face-to-face meeting with a foreign general deep within the Imperial Palace was an indication of where things stood for the Japanese and Hirohito.
https://en.wikipedia.org/wiki/File:Macarthur_hirohito.jpg

One of the first issues that had to be tackled by the Allies was the prosecution of accused Japanese war criminals. It was made quite clear that the emperor would not be put on trial. Many Americans and Allies whose soldiers and civilians had suffered so greatly at the hands of the Japanese were infuriated by the idea, but by the time the International Military Tribunal for the Far East convened in April 1946 in Tokyo, most opposition to the emperor's immunity was limited to the more extreme parts of the Allied body politic. Most knew that if the emperor were put on trial, the Japanese would likely rise up against the occupation. While the uprising would not likely have succeeded, it would surely have been bloody. Even before the announcement that Hirohito would be retained as emperor, many Japanese officers had killed themselves rather than live with the dishonor that would bring.

The Tokyo War Crimes Tribunal was only one of the war crimes tribunals that took place in nations formerly occupied by Japan. The Tokyo proceedings put the top surviving Japanese military and civilian leaders in the dock. Twenty-eight civilian and military leaders, including General Tojo, who had led Japan through much of the war, were accused of crimes ranging from "aggressive war" to forced labor, torture, murder, and mass murder, which were all considered crimes against humanity.

The trial lasted a year and a half, and when it was over, seven men (Tojo among them) were sentenced to death. Sixteen were sentenced to life in prison. Two others had died from natural causes in custody, and one was deemed unfit to stand trial. The Tokyo trials were only the main proceedings carried out in the prosecution of war crimes. In the Philippines, for instance, General Yamashita was found guilty of war crimes and executed in 1946.

In Europe, many Nazis known to be war criminals escaped justice. Some of them were aided and abetted by the Allies, particularly the US and the USSR, since they wanted access to possible German intelligence about each other and knowledge of advanced German scientific studies (some of which had involved war crimes themselves). This information did not become widespread public knowledge until the late 1970s and 1980s, and when it did, it caused outrage, at least in the US. Unfortunately, many Japanese war criminals, possibly including the heads of some of the larger Japanese corporations (many large Japanese companies forced prisoners of war to work for them under appalling conditions that they both knew about and created), were overlooked when it came to the war crimes trials, at least in Japan.

One of the most notorious criminals of the war, in both Asia and Europe, was the commander of the infamous Japanese "Unit 731," which had conducted "medical experiments" and torture in their headquarters in Manchuria. Its commander, Surgeon General Ishii, had devised and overseen chemical and biological warfare experiments on the Chinese population and Allied prisoners of war, including a number of pilots from the famed Doolittle Raid who had crashed in China after dropping their bombs on Tokyo. Estimates of the deaths caused by Ishii and his unit approached half a million or more. Sadly, the Americans, who held him in custody, determined the knowledge that Ishii possessed might be useful to them, especially since they would never be able to carry out the types of sadistic experiments that he did. Ishii was a monster almost without rival, and he died in 1957, having been given immunity from prosecution.

The first year of the American occupation was bleak for Japan, though the nightmares of many Japanese did not come true—there was no American wave of revenge, murder, and rape, though it's likely that it did happen on a wider scale than was officially reported. Still, all things considered, the occupation began and ended relatively peacefully. At first, to avoid the feared wave of violence expected from the Americans, the Japanese set up what they called "comfort stations" for the American troops. The result of this was an epidemic of venereal diseases. When word got back to the US, politicians, wives, and mothers put pressure on MacArthur to end this practice. In their place, the Japanese set up legal brothels, where US troops had to pay for "comfort."

Starvation hit parts of Japan, and there were thousands of deaths from hunger. Most of the crops went to the larger cities, but even that was insufficient. There was simply a lack of manpower. For the first year of the US occupation, organized crime filled in the gaps that the American administration had not yet reached or could not reach. Thievery was rampant, and at times, American officers were forced to pay criminals for their own goods. American occupation and the 1950s were the heyday for the infamous Japanese "mafia," the Yakuza.

However, for many, there were opportunities. The Americans needed translators, even those whose English skills were not very good. These translators often played a dual role. Not only did they translate, but they also knew the ins and outs of Japanese society and who could get things done. Entrepreneurs and people who wished to help rebuild Japan's economy also found opportunities, for American money and advisers were pouring into the country.

There are a number of ways to analyze America's role in the world after WWII, especially as it relates to Japan and Germany. Most historians believed that the main US motive was to rebuild those countries as democratic nations. There is certainly a level of truth to that. Many of those same historians also postulate that while America wished to promote democracy in both Germany and Japan, there was also a desire to build strong bulwarks against Soviet communism in Europe and Asia. There was also certainly an element of humanitarianism in the American effort as well.

The goals of democratizing and rebuilding Japan and Germany went hand in hand. With a democratic government in power and America rebuilding their industries, both Japan and Germany would be impediments to the spread of communism desired by the Soviet Union.

In Europe, the US had little choice. The Soviets occupied roughly half of Germany, and the USSR had suffered more at the hands of the Nazis than anyone else. However, the war against Japan was dominated by the Americans. Thus, Japan was fully occupied by the Americans, and the US had absolutely no intention of allowing the Soviet Union any say or influence in Japan, despite the Soviets claiming they had launched a massive attack on Japanese forces in China. This came in the war's last days and was hardly necessary for the defeat of Japan.

One reason for American intransigence over any Soviet role in Japan was geopolitical. For fifty years, the United States had been establishing supply stations and possessions in the Pacific to protect their business interests and support the US Navy there. The occupation of Japan (and the later treaties that established a permanent US military presence in the country) provided the

United States with an "unsinkable aircraft carrier" and a military base in the Pacific. Japan lay in close proximity to China, the Soviet Union, and Korea.

With the end of Japan's occupation of much of China, the civil war that had begun there before the Japanese arrived in 1937 once again broke out into an open, bloody conflict. The Soviets supported the Chinese Communists under Mao Zedong, and the US supported Nationalist leader Chiang Kai-shek. Japan was a convenient staging area for American supplies going to China. The loss of China to the Communists in 1949 only made the American occupation of Japan more important.

The other crucial area of Asia in the late 1940s was Korea. Korea, like Germany, had been divided into two nations after the defeat of the occupying Japanese. The North became communist under Kim Il-Sung, a patron of both the Soviet Union and Mao Zedong, and the South became an American client state governed by the autocratic president Syngman Rhee. As you may know, the communist North, with the support of both China and the Soviet Union, invaded the South in 1950. Without the staging and resupply bases in Japan, the American effort in Korea might have been in vain.

There is a reason this section of the book seems more about MacArthur and the United States. The United States and its general remade Japan in many ways. MacArthur had a two-step plan for post-war Japan: demilitarization and democratization. As you now know, for most of Japan's history, it was dominated by the military, or at least the military force of one daimyo or another. Until the Meiji Restoration, Japan had no experience with any sort of democratic rule. Even the governments of the Meiji era were top-down regimes, though a parliament did debate the issues of the day.

MacArthur and most American policy-makers knew that the military had been the source of Japan's problems for many years. Before the outbreak of war in China, the military consumed 75 percent of Japan's entire budget, and it drove policy. Within days of being in Japan. MacArthur decreed the end of the Japanese military. This was not only earth-shaking historically but also logistically as well, for millions of Japanese soldiers were still in China, Indochina, Korea, Indonesia, New Guinea, and elsewhere.

Even in China, where most Japanese prisoners fell under Allied control and received decent treatment, Japanese soldiers were malnourished, sick, and tired of war. The Imperial Japanese Navy's defeat at the hands of the US and the destruction of its merchant fleet meant that many Japanese starved to death. There were documented cases of cannibalism even before the war ended. (One of the most amazing documentary films ever, *The Emperor's Naked Army Marches On*, discusses the subject. For those of you familiar with Japanese culture, this movie will be a revelation.) The seven million Japanese soldiers who were stationed in China would eventually form a large part of the workforce that would rebuild Japan in 2022, which has the third-largest economy in the world after the United States and China as of this publication.

The next steps in demilitarization were crucial. As you read earlier, the Japanese secret police were part of the military. The *Kempeitai*, which literally means "Law Soldier Regiment" but was more commonly referred to as the "thought police," had turned Japan into a totalitarian state. It was perhaps even more pervasive than what had existed in the Soviet Union and Nazi Germany, and it was aided by the Japanese people's history and the idea of social harmony in Japanese culture. MacArthur disbanded the *Kempeitai* when he eliminated the military. Anyone stained with suspicion of a war crime was also removed. A considerable number of secret police officers were forced into criminality, and the Yakuza formed because of these decrees, though most eventually found a place in society.

MacArthur (and, through him, his headquarters and the American military government) was known by the acronym SCAP for "Supreme Commander for the Allied Powers." SCAP and the Americans knew about the monopoly-like conglomerates, the *zaibatsu*. For decades, Japanese politics was influenced and corrupted by the power and money of the *zaibatsu*, which, along with the military, controlled offices in government administration and had parliament members in their pockets. The Americans ordered land reform, as well as the breaking up of monopolies and their reconstruction into their less-monolithic form, the *keiretsu*. The *keiretsu* still carried more traits of large trusts and monopolies than most Americans would be comfortable with. You will recognize some of these names, as they are still among the largest and richest companies in the world: Nissan, Fuji, Mitsubishi, Sumitomo. Others, such as Sony and Toyota, began after the war.

The Americans realized that Japan's experiment with democracy in the late 1800s and early 1900s was based on a European parliamentary government, so they did not try to replace it with the American two-party system. The Americans attempted to create new parties based on Western democratic ideals and tried to purge many of the older pre-war politicians and organizations. They were only partly successful, for many of the older politicians still had influence, and the two main political parties that emerged after the war—the Liberal Democratic Party ("LDP") and the Progressive Party—were basically two of the pre-war parties with different names.

This brings up an interesting problem the Americans faced. The occupation of Japan could not have really gone any smoother for either the Japanese or the Americans, especially considering the cost of the war in both lives and money and the brutality with which it was fought. The Americans did have the power to impose their will on the Japanese, and they likely could have completely broken up the *zaibatsu* and made political reforms, but that would spark revolts and possibly allow communism to enter and spread.

You have read how Hirohito was kept on as a unifying figure, one that could help keep Japan peaceful. This was also the case with the political parties and the *zaibatsu*. Either of those entities could have caused a lot of problems for SCAP. It should also be noted that though the economy did show signs of recovery by the end of the 1940s, times in Japan after the war were exceedingly difficult. Many laborers, ex-soldiers, and the unemployed began to look toward communism as the answer to Japan's economic problems. The Americans, the *zaibatsu*, the old politicians, and even the Yakuza did not want this, so SCAP compromised and looked the other way to a degree.

What they would not compromise on were guarantees of fundamental human rights, the elimination of the military (that would change as the Soviet Union and China became bigger threats in the 1950s), and a new democratic constitution with checks and balances on power. SCAP also reformed the education system to promote free thought and democratic principles, removed laws against most censorship (especially of words and films critical of the government), and secured the right for unions to exist and the right to strike in Japan. These were monumental changes and were largely accomplished during the administration of Douglas MacArthur, who was famously called the "American Caesar" for his role in winning the war and reshaping Japan.

Minorities

From the outside, it may seem that the people of Japan are, well, all ethnic Japanese. That is not the case, but one could not be blamed for believing it because for centuries, successive governments of Japan, from the Tokugawa to the military dictatorship and even to the democratic governments since the war, have either encouraged that belief openly or tacitly encouraged it.

During the war, the government and military frequently spoke of the "national harmony and strength" of the Japanese people. By "Japanese people," they meant the dominant ethnic group, the Yamato Japanese, the people most readily identified as Japanese and who make up about 95 percent of the citizens of Japan today. As far as foreigners living in Japan go, that amounted to about 2 to 3 percent for quite a long time, though in Tokyo, that figure is closer to 10 percent. As one might expect, most of the foreign nationals living in Japan come from nearby nations, such as China, South Korea, Vietnam, and the Philippines. The foreigners living in Japan generally fall into three categories: white-collar businessmen, shopkeepers and tradesmen, and manual laborers, most often domestic workers such as hotel maids.

That leaves about 2 percent of the population, which amounts to roughly 2.5 million people. Who are these people? They are Japan's native ethnic minorities. Perhaps the most well-known are the Ainu people of the northernmost main island of Japan, Hokkaido. The Ainu have lived in Hokkaido since before recorded time. Since the war and the democratization of the country, many Ainu people have intermarried with the dominant Japanese Yamato. Some estimates of people identifying solely as Ainu are as low as 25,000 and go as high as 200,000.

The Ainu are distinct from their countrymen in a number of ways. They tend to be smaller in stature, and the males generally have thicker facial hair (more traditional men often sport a thick beard). However, the most distinct thing about the Ainu is that most of them practice a native animist religion, akin in many ways to the native peoples of Siberia and North America. For centuries, the Ainu were semi-nomadic hunter-gatherers, like many native tribes around the world.

Until the 1800s, Hokkaido was mainly a trading place for the Japanese. The Ainu (sometimes disparagingly called "the hairy Ainu" by the Japanese) were left to themselves, trading furs, fish, and sometimes ivory with their southern "cousins." That changed in the Meiji era when Hokkaido, with its mountainous terrain and rough weather, began to be settled and modernized.

For quite some time, there were attempts to suppress the Ainus' native beliefs and convert them to the dominant spiritual beliefs of Japan, Shintoism and Buddhism. But the refusal of many Ainu and the spread of liberal ideas after the war ended those attempts.

Japan's next largest minority are the Ryukuans, whose name comes from the Ryukyu Islands, which lay about halfway between mainland Japan and Taiwan. You likely know of the main island in the chain, Okinawa. Though the Ryukyu Kingdom was taken over by the Tokugawa in 1600, the island chain did not become part of Japan until 1879.

Perhaps the most well-known fact about Okinawa, aside from the tremendous battle that took place there in 1945, is that karate was developed there. Karate means "open-hand" and was originally called *bushi no te* or "the hands of the gentleman warrior." The martial art slowly developed over the centuries, but its present form was a reaction to the unification of the Ryukyus under one dynasty in 1507. As in mainland Japan, the dynasty forbade the population from carrying weapons, so "open-hand" was perfected instead. Teaching karate was even forbidden after the annexation of the Ryukyus by the Tokugawa. Of course, karate lessons continued anyway.

In Japan, Okinawans have generally been regarded as sort of the "hillbillies" of the nation. They have a distinct dialect and are different from mainland Japanese society in many ways, though over the years, especially since the war, these differences have become less stark.

The Japanese have had a history of treating the Ainu and the people of the Ryukyus with a subtle disdain. For many years, unemployment and educational opportunities were difficult for those people.

Burakumin

The Burakumin are Japanese, but even today, especially among the older generations of Japan, they are often looked down upon. The reason is unusual, at least for outsiders. Traditional Japanese beliefs, incorporated in both Shinto and Buddhist beliefs, view working with death or dead things as distasteful. Death symbolizes decay, and the preferred method of the disposal of dead bodies is cremation.

Related to that, at least in the past, was one's diet. The Japanese, except for the Ainu, did not eat meat. The raising of cattle, pigs, and other livestock takes up a lot of space, which Japan does not have. Secondly, the handling of dead flesh (excluding fish), whether that of animals or humans, was considered a form of contamination. Still, there was a need for it; leather was needed, plow animals and horses died, and people died. Someone had to do it. These people are known as the Burakumin today. Until the latter part of the 20th century, many Japanese referred to the Burakumin as "Eta" or "filth eaters" because, being the poorest of the poor, these people often ate the entrails (offal) of dead animals. "Burakumin" translates into "people of the village or hamlet," for they often lived in poor huts and settlements in larger cities. Westerners would refer to these villages as a ghetto.

Though today many people descended from Burakumin families have been assimilated into Japanese society, there is still a stigma attached to the Burakumin by various segments, such as the elite political class, many older Japanese, and ultra-nationalists.

For centuries, population records, which became increasingly exact from the Tokugawa period onward, were kept by Shinto priests and monks at local shrines. Every so many years, a national census would be taken, and those records would have to be condensed for the government. In those records, the location and number of Burakumin would be noted. This was not only a way of calculating population but also for a family to determine whether their son or daughter was marrying into a Burakumin family.

Even today, there are some families that pay investigators to find out whether their prospective son-in-law or daughter-in-law is Burakumin. Many Shinto shrines destroyed their records to prevent this kind of discrimination from happening, but the information can often be found by looking hard enough. The internet has made hiring these detectives easier.

Though there have been increasing numbers of Burakumin and non-Burakumin marriages, unfortunately, a number of engagements have ended in suicide pacts. Some have occurred relatively recently—you can find a link for an article about one such occurrence in the bibliography.

Many Japanese are curious about the racial and ethnic tensions in America. The initial questions are usually something along the lines of "We don't have such problems in Japan." But the truth is, they do—it just looks different and is not as well known. Most Burakumin still live in relatively insular communities, with most living in the biggest cities. The Burakumin population is estimated at about 1.2 million people.

The Burakumin have faced discrimination getting non-traditional Burakumin jobs and often do not have the same access to social services as other Japanese. As a result, research has shown that about 60 percent of Yakuza members have roots in Burakumin families, which, ironically, causes more of the discrimination that forces people into a life of crime in the first place.

Though there are now Burakumin rights groups that lobby local and national governments for better treatment, as well as Burakumin-descended politicians, as recently as the early 2000s, a number of scandals erupted, including one in which a candidate for prime minister was "outed" as Burakumin. He decided not to run for the position. Still, considering the centuries-long discrimination against the Burakumin, much has changed, but despite the claims of many Japanese inside and outside the government, much work needs to be done.

The Constitution of 1947

Though much groundwork had been laid to bring change to the Japanese political system, the ultimate development was the new Japanese constitution. Initially, SCAP wanted the Japanese to be the pointmen in the creation of this new document and appointed a renowned Japanese legal scholar to form a committee to debate and create a new constitution. Unfortunately for those on the committee, their work proved unacceptable to MacArthur and most of the other Allies. It included articles that allowed the emperor to retain much power (though he was "encouraged" not to use it), stating that the officials of the government should offer advice to the emperor, who would then endorse it. As you can probably guess, MacArthur and the American government gave that arrangement a hard no. Instead, a man named Courtney Whitney, who was the head of the US government section of SCAP's staff, was assigned to literally write Japan a new constitution. That very document, with some minor changes, is the Constitution of Japan today.

The most well-known part of that constitution is Article 9, which prohibits Japan from developing an army, navy, or other armed force. After the American military occupation of Japan ended in 1952, Article 9 was interpreted to mean that Japan should have a self-defense force but not an armed force that could wage offensive wars. It also forbids Japan from sending troops anywhere other than Japanese possessions. The Americans were happy to supervise the building, training, and equipping of the JDF (Japanese Defense Force) because the troops stationed in Japan could be used in other places in the increasingly tense Cold War with the Soviet Union and China. There are around thirty thousand men in the JDF today.

During the 2010s, former Prime Minister Abe Shinzo and his successor, Kishida Fumio (remember, last name first), pushed for an expanded Japanese armed force and increased roles in some of the hot spots around the world. This is now supported by the United States and other Western countries, as Japan is increasingly at odds with China over a number of small islands called the Senkakus in Japan and Diaoyu in China.

The Constitution of 1947, in addition to guaranteeing equal rights (at least in theory) to minorities, also codified equal rights for women. The story of the struggle for women's rights in Japan is long, and any discussion of the issue that would do it justice would be much longer than this introductory book. There are two very good books in the bibliography about women's rights and their evolution in Japan, which we encourage you to check out.

For our purposes here, most historians and sociologists would say there has been much progress in the advancement of women's rights in Japan, but all too often, they are honored in the breach. For many years, until it drew increasing notice from the press in both Japan and overseas, a "token" woman might be on the board of a large business or corporation, but in most instances, her position, while paid, was just for show. That has begun to change in the 21st century, as more and more women have entered the workforce in positions of responsibility and excelled. Increasing numbers of women have become involved in politics on a local, provincial, and national level, which has provoked a significant amount of change.

Chapter 8 – "Economic Miracle"

In 1986, Paramount Pictures released the Ron Howard-directed movie *Gung Ho* with rising star Michael Keaton. The movie told the story of a small town whose car factory was being bought by a fictional Japanese automobile company. The Japanese who come to manage the plant hire Hunt Stevenson (played by Michael Keaton), a foreman popular with the workers, to be a kind of liaison between labor and management. Soon, Keaton's character finds himself between two sides in a culture war within the plant.

The Japanese insist on exercising in the morning for team-building and installing a strict regime of time management to improve production and to catch mistakes made on the assembly line. Naturally, both sides are caricatured, with the Americans being wild and lazy and the Japanese being too task-driven at the expense of their humanity. In the middle of this are Keaton and "Kaz" Kazuhiro, the executive sent by Japan to turn the plant around. Both find things about the other's culture at first maddening, then surprisingly effective. By the end of the film, the two are working together.

The movie was relatively successful and a fictional example of the many American businesses (and real estate) being bought by the Japanese in the 1980s. Many Americans got the idea that the Japanese were buying the whole country and that even the local mom-and-pop stores would be owned by someone from Japan. Of course, that was all overblown. However, the idea that the Japanese would soon be selling more cars in the US than Ford and GM panicked many people.

By the late 1980s and early 1990s, it did seem as if the Japanese were buying up much of America. It seemed as if America's industries were falling behind the efficient, organized, and unified investors from Asia. But how did that happen?

The Japanese "Economic Miracle," as the recovery from WWII is almost always referred to, happened between the early 1950s and 1970s. By the 1980s, Japan was among the most prosperous and industrially advanced nations in the world.

Japan was, of course, devastated by the war. Millions were dead or wounded, and millions of soldiers were coming home with few job opportunities waiting for them. Hunger stalked the country. Bad weather, combined with the loss of labor and infrastructure, along with the loss of Taiwanese and Korean rice production, all contributed to the problem. America sent grain, new rice hybrids, and more than a billion and a half dollars (twenty-four billion today when adjusted for inflation) to aid Japan between 1946 and 1950.

This aid, while stemming the tide of starvation, also contributed to inflation, which was made worse by the new Japanese government unwisely printing too much money. Attempts to control prices were ineffective, reaching over 300 percent in 1946 and coming down to only 63 percent in 1949. The American Dodge Plan, which helped contain the production and flow of currency, finally began to get inflation under control, but the Japanese needed to act fast, not only for the sake of their countrymen but also to avoid a rise in the increasing number of Japanese drawn to communism.

The Ministry of International Trade and Industry (MITI) was the Japanese government agency largely responsible for turning things around and getting Japan's economy back on track. In the years immediately after the war, the only things in the Japanese export market were trinkets and poorly made traditional Japanese sketches, cheap paintings, and geisha dolls. They were known for being shoddy and were so pervasive after the war, especially as millions of American soldiers passed through Japan in the late 1940s and early 1950s, that Japanese-made products had a thoroughly undeserved reputation for bad quality for a long time.

To turn this situation around, MITI took a number of important steps. Like the Japanese had during the early Meiji era, it sent thousands of men abroad to learn current Western management styles, industrial techniques, factories, and much else. It also provided low-interest loans to companies in major industries, as these industries would be needed for Japan to build its industrial base and begin to export products that were wanted and needed overseas.

The beneficiaries of most of these loans were mainly the former *zaibatsu* companies in the heavy industry, but a number of new companies appeared as well, such as Sony, Honda, and Toyota—all household names in the world today. Contributing to the success of these companies was the work ethic of the Japanese. From executives to workers on the factory floor, men and women (who were slowly making up a larger part of the workforce) put in long days and long weeks. Though unions were legal, there were very few strikes since this would put a dent in production and cause management to crack down, either through the loss of jobs or intimidation. In return for their industry, both white- and blue-collar workers received lifetime employment, increasingly generous retirement pensions, and medical insurance, among other things.

In 1960, the MITI and the government introduced a plan for doubling the size of the economy in ten years. Continued tax breaks for large companies and very large but very specific government investments (in the auto industry, for example) were made to help increase production, which was largely for export at first. Very few Japanese could afford a car until the later 1960s and 1970s.

Another important industry that benefited from these loans was the railroad industry. Trains had been popular in Japan since the arrival of Commodore Perry. Knowing that trade depended on shipping goods in a timely way and that conveying more people into the cities was good for the economy, a massive railroad building program began. The pinnacle of this development was the Shinkansen or "bullet train," which was deployed in Japan in 1964, far before anything similar was built in the US or Europe. The development of the bullet train, which is still a point of pride in Japan, was a sign that the Japanese had not only recovered but also surpassed the West in certain areas.

The growth target of the income-doubling plan was a 7.5 percent increase in annual economic growth. In actuality, the growth of Japan's economy surpassed 10 percent for the entire time, and Japan's income doubled in less than seven years, not ten.

Another major factor in the recovery of the economy was land reform. This began under SCAP and continued after the occupation authority handed complete power back to the Japanese government. Large landowners were forced to sell all but one of their holdings. In turn, the government sold much of this land to tenant farmers who had been living and working on that land for years. By 1950, nearly 40 percent of Japan's arable land was sold in this manner, and families who had never owned their own land for centuries had become stakeholders in the country's economy. Government programs, as well as aid and technology from the United States, turned Japan's agricultural system into one that could not only support the growing population but also allow for the export of a limited but growing amount of Japanese agricultural products. (Today, Japan's population is in decline, presenting its own economic and social problems.)

The Japanese are rightly proud of the economic miracle, which took them from utter devastation to the third-largest economy in the world. Until the rise of China, Japan was often the world's second-largest economy. Still, it must be said the protection and contribution of the United States made this miracle possible, at least in part.

For much of the Cold War, the Japanese Defense Force was a small and underdeveloped national guard. No one outside Japan wanted to see a renewed and powerful Japanese army and navy. In the 1950s, 1960s, and 1970s (and even into the 80s and 90s), the Japanese did not need a large or powerful armed service. They had the Americans to protect them. Major US airbases dotted Japan, the Pacific Fleet was headquartered there, and US Marine and Army bases dotted the country, especially Okinawa. (Conflicts between Okinawans and US Marines over US military crimes, such as assault and rape, led to protests against the US presence and problems between the governments.) Japan was an armed fortress, and it was armed with American personnel and equipment.

This was not an issue for the United States for much of the post-war period. America was more than happy with the arrangement. The US had a forward base in Asia, and the Japanese could (and did) take the money they would have spent on arms and use it for domestic economic development. This amounted to hundreds of billions of dollars over time.

Today, the Japanese are debating an increased role in military efforts, especially since China has become more aggressive in the Pacific. The relationship between the US and Japan is one of the closest on Earth, and America has been encouraging the strong and large Japanese Defense Force. But overseas deployment and an expansion of the armed forces would require not only changes in Japan's constitution but also a fundamental shift in the way that Japan thinks about its place in the world.

The End of the Miracle and the End of an Era

For the last ten or so years, Japan's economic growth has been roughly 2 to 3 percent a year. In the 1990s, a number of issues contributed to a serious downturn in the Japanese economy. Inflated prices (especially in real estate), bad loans, and increasingly expensive business models (such as lifetime employment) all caused the Japanese economy to go into recession. This was not unique to Japan at the time, but for a country used to constant economic advancement since 1950, the recession of the mid-1990s to the 2010s came as quite a shock. For the first time in memory, cities in Japan, especially Tokyo, saw homelessness on a large scale. Unfortunately, many of the homeless were elderly people whose dream of lifetime employment ended in unbelievably neat homeless villages in the subway systems of the country, which were erected in the late evening and disappeared for the morning rush.

As of this writing, Japan is faced with a labor crisis. Their workforce and population are aging, and there has been much debate and cost-cutting within the economy as to what path to take to restore at least a semblance of the famous "Economic Miracle."

In 1971, Emperor Hirohito visited the United States and met with President Richard Nixon; he was the first emperor to ever leave the shores of Japan. The visit garnered international attention, and many Americans, especially those of the WWII generation, were not happy with the visit of a man who had (at the very least) knowledge of widespread war crimes. Still, the visit illustrated to the world, especially to China and the Soviet Union, the closeness of the two democratic countries and how far they had come since the war.

Hirohito died in 1989, and his son, Akihito, became the next emperor. Akihito was seen as more of a "man of the people," and he and his very popular wife, Empress Michiko, were seen in public to a greater degree than any of Akihito's predecessors combined. In 2019, Akihito abdicated in favor of his son, Naruhito, due to ill health. To show how far things have come, Naruhito's wife, Masako, is a commoner, though she had a career and a Harvard degree before she became empress. She is quite popular but is said to struggle with her time in the public eye.

Conclusion

We hope you have enjoyed this book on modern Japan. Japanese history is incredibly detailed, rich, and interesting. By necessity, much has been left out to give the broadest picture possible of a history that is unlike any other in the world.

Twice in less than one hundred years, the Japanese completely rebuilt their country. No other nation, with the possible exception of 21st-century China, had come so far, so fast. From a nation consisting of wooden buildings governed by sword-wielding warriors right out of the 1600s to a surprise world power and short-lived empire, Japan defied all expectations.

The resilience of the Japanese was shown again when the Tohoku earthquake, the most powerful to ever hit Japan, caused a deadly tsunami that resulted in the failure of the Fukushima Daichi nuclear plant in 2011. This, in turn, caused the shutdown of the plant and the creation of a large irradiated "no-go" zone on the northeastern coast of the largest Japanese island, Honshu.

The reaction of the government and the nuclear energy company was widely criticized as being slow, secretive, and perhaps corrupt. At the very least, the reaction stirred Japanese fears of a nuclear disaster and of the secretive male-dominated bureaucracies that had partly controlled Japan behind the scenes during the "Economic Miracle." There have been massive lawsuits and legislative changes as a result of the disasters, and hopefully, a more responsive national and corporate bureaucracy is being created.

Japan is one of the most influential countries in the world. This is mainly economic in nature, but since the end of the war, Japanese movies, cartoons, food, and artistic styles have spread worldwide. Today, Japanese or Japanese-inspired anime and manga are exceedingly popular and emulated the world over. Kawaii ("cute") culture is a Japanese phenomenon that is becoming increasingly universal in its appeal.

Illustration 31: An example of kawaii fashion.
Lrn carrozza, CC BY-SA 3.0 <https://creativecommons.org/licenses/by-sa/3.0>, via Wikimedia Commons; https://en.wikipedia.org/wiki/File:Kawaii_Fashion.jpg

Japan has greatly influenced the world, and it is likely this will continue in the future.

Here's another book by Captivating History that you might like

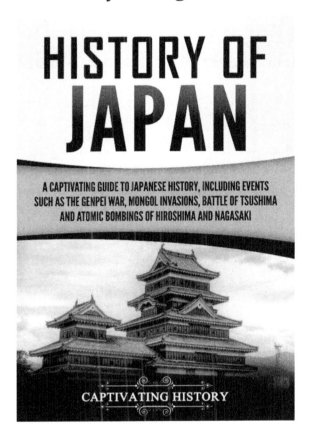

Free Bonus from Captivating History (Available for a Limited time)

Hi History Lovers!

Now you have a chance to join our exclusive history list so you can get your first history ebook for free as well as discounts and a potential to get more history books for free! Simply visit the link below to join.

Captivatinghistory.com/ebook

Also, make sure to follow us on Facebook, Twitter and Youtube by searching for Captivating History.

Bibliography

Bardsley, Jan. *Women and Democracy in Cold War Japan.* 2014.

Clavell, James. *Shōgun.* London: Hodder & Stoughton, 1975.

The Emperor's Naked Army Marches On. Directed by Hara Kazuo. n.d. Tokyo, 1987. Film.

Dear, Ian, I. C. Dear, and M. R. Foot. *Oxford Companion to World War II.* Oxford: OUP Oxford, 2001.

Evans, David C., and Mark R. Peattie. *Kaigun: Strategy, Tactics, and Technology in the Imperial Japanese Navy, 1887-1941.* Naval Inst Press, 2012.

Gaulkin, Thomas. "Counting the Dead at Hiroshima and Nagasaki." Bulletin of the Atomic Scientists. Last modified September 17, 2020. https://thebulletin.org/2020/08/counting-the-dead-at-hiroshima-and-nagasaki/.

Gnam, Carl. "The Kempeitai: Japan's Dreaded 'Gestapo.'" Warfare History Network. Last modified May 6, 2020. https://warfarehistorynetwork.com/the-kempeitai-japans-dreaded-gestapo/.

Farkas, Ivan. "Hiroshima 'Shadows' And 4 Other Haunting Historical Remnants." Cracked.com. Last modified October 21, 2016. https://www.cracked.com/article_24402_hiroshima-shadows-4-other-haunting-historical-remnants.html.

Hardacre, Helen. *Shinto.* New York: Oxford University Press, 2016.

The Independent. "Shogun: The Facts Behind the Fiction." The Independent. Last modified May 5, 2005. https://www.independent.co.uk/news/uk/this-britain/shogun-the-facts-behind-the-fiction-236933.html.

Lebra, Joyce C., and Taylor & Francis Group. *Women in Changing Japan*. London: Routledge, 2020.

Manchester, William. *American Caesar: Douglas MacArthur 1880–1964*. Back Bay Books, 2008.

Packard, George R. *Edwin O. Reischauer and the American Discovery of Japan*. New York: Columbia University Press, 2010.

Reischauer, Edwin O. *Japan, Past & Present: By Edwin O. Reischauer*. 1964.

"Tokugawa Ieyasu." Japan Experience, a Unique Experience | Japan Experience. Accessed May 25, 2022. https://www.japan-experience.com/plan-your-trip/to-know/japanese-history/tokugawa-ieyasu.

"What and who are the Buraku and Burakumin."

"The Rise and Fall of the Japanese Miracle | Jeffrey M. Herbener." Mises Institute. Accessed July 25, 2022. https://mises.org/library/rise-and-fall-japanese-miracle.

Printed in Great Britain
by Amazon

18981226R00088